THE SEARCH FOR SCHOLARSHIPS

The Andrews System: A Step-by-Step Guide
to Finding Money for College

EVE-MARIE ANDREWS

The Search for Scholarships
The Andrews System: A Step-by-Step Guide
to Finding Money for College

Second Edition — Fall 2019

Dedication

To my students past and present, who have motivated me to make scholarships my purpose in life. From them I have learned to be a better counselor and a better teacher. By sharing what I have learned about finding money for college, I have been privileged to be a part of many lives. Their successes become mine and each time a scholarship is awarded, my spirits are uplifted.

Although all of my students are very special people, I must confess that I have four favorites who call me Vavoa, Portuguese for grandmother. I love you guys. You are my reason for living.

David Andrew Westengard
Jordyn Elizabeth Andrade
Jonmarie Ann Westengard
Jared William Andrade

Table of Contents

Getting Started

The cost of attending college keeps rising. This year the average annual tuition at an Ivy League College (Harvard, Yale, Princeton) is $51,397 (and Stanford) is $54,414. In addition, there are books and supplies, transportation, and room and board.

The national average for tuition plus books and supplies at a two-year public college is $3,660; for a four-year public college, it is $6,778; and for a four-year private college, it is $35,830.

The average student owes $29,900. Many undergraduates though, have debt exceeding $40,000. (A young man I know who is about fifty-eight years old still owes about $89,000 in student loans.) He received a master's degree thirty years ago.

That's just wrong! For the last twenty-three years, my main purpose as a community college counselor and instructor has been not only to make students and their parents aware of the billions of dollars that are available to students wanting to go to college, but also to teach them how to apply successfully for scholarships and to win them!

One of my students recently won about $75,000 in scholarships. Yes, she is a single parent and a serious student, but the reason for her success is that she used **The Andrews System.** With my time management and organization tips and techniques, her scholarship portfolio is so complete that she can submit an application within a twenty-four hour deadline.

Many students have the notion that in order to qualify for a scholarship you must have a 4.0 GPA and/or be financially destitute. This is not always true! There are thousand of scholarships available based on other factors, and many awards for average students.

Granted it does take time to complete an application, and preparing all of the necessary documents can be tedious, but once your portfolio is completed, you are ready to apply for any and all awards. The small scholarships add up — it is foolish to concentrate only on the large awards. The larger the scholarship, the more competition you will encounter.

By using **The Andrews System** you can streamline the application process and complete in hours what would have taken days or weeks. The result is you can apply to more places, increasing your odds significantly.

Many of my students have received seven and eight scholarships that add up to thousands of dollars. The money is out there, and it is yours for the applying, but you must be willing to put in the effort and follow the system. It works!

Putting in a couple of hours to complete an application toward a $2,500 scholarship makes more financial sense than working a whole month for half that amount. I'm not suggesting that you quit your job, but know that if you follow **The Andrews System** and keep applying, the odds are good that you will receive some form of financial aid.

I have devoted my life to helping as many students as I can win scholarships. This is my area of expertise and I know that thousands of organizations want to help you, but you have to let them know that you are the deserving candidate. Come on, **think scholarships, and think "YOU WANT TO GIVE TO ME".**

Now let's talk about how to get it...

Section 1
Working the System

Let's Go!

Have It on Hand

Creating Your Portfolio

Assembling Your Portfolio

1

Notes

Let's Go!

OK, you are ready to take the first steps toward winning lots of money for college. By now, you know that there are thousands of opportunities for someone like you and they all have one thing in common. Paperwork! The old saying goes, "you can't get something for nothing" and it's true. There is work involved, but our goal is to make it possible for you to find a scholarship that fits your profile and then turn around the paperwork in a matter of hours.

By having your portfolio complete, you will have all of the necessary documents to complete scholarship applications in record time. By setting things up according to **The Andrews System,** you can apply for at least 100 scholarships a year. Impossible? No, that is less than two a week.

The Key to The Andrews System is Organization

Have It On Hand

The more you apply, the more you make and there is nothing more frustrating than finding a generous award and not having the materials on hand to meet the deadline. So, let's take a look at some of the documentation that scholarship offices look for and how to get them.

Note:

Not all scholarship applications require ALL of the following documents, but you will want them available at a moment's notice.

◆ Transcripts

These are printed copies of your high school and college grades. Most scholarship applications will want a copy of your **official transcripts.** In order to be official they must remain in the sealed envelope in which they were received.

For high school transcripts, you can start off by asking a counselor what the procedure is at your specific school. For college transcripts, check with the Admissions and Records office or the Registrar's office.

Some colleges have adopted a new procedure for requesting transcripts which entails contacting a private organization. Since this may involve a bit more time, having at least one copy in your portfolio is to your advantage.

◆ SAT Scores

This is a standardized test for college admissions which high schools administer to the senior class. If you need a copy of the results, or if you would like to make arrangements to take the SAT, you can contact *www.CollegeBoard.com.*

◆ Tax Returns

A tax return is a form on which you must give details of your income and expenses. The tax return is then used to calculate the amount of tax that you are due to pay. Taxpayers receive a copy in the mail, but the form is available online through *www.irs.gov/formpubs/index.htm.*

◆ The FAFSA Form (Free Application for Student Aid)

Most states and schools use FAFSA information to award their financial aid. Your responses are entered into a formula to determine eligibility. Eligibility is based on income and ability to pay. EVERYONE should apply even if you don't think you qualify. It is so important there is a whole chapter devoted to it later on in this book.

It is more expedient to apply online — it is 14% more accurate and you receive the results in days rather than weeks. To access the application form, please go to *www.FAFSA.ed.gov.* For greater efficiency, download the worksheet (pre-application form) so that you have all of the information that you need in front of you when you actually complete the FAFSA application.

A word of caution!!!

*If you accidentally type in .com instead of .ed.gov, you will get a service that offers to complete the form for you for a fee of $79.99. **Remember!** It is a **FREE APPLICATION**. Should you need any assistance in completing the form, a counselor or someone in the Financial Aid Office will be happy to help you.*

Scholarship applications will usually require a FAFSA Student Aid Report (SAR) or tax return.

◆ SAR (Student Aid Report)

This report is generated from the FAFSA application. The college uses this to determine your financial aid. Scholarship applications will usually require a copy of your W-2 Forms, 1099 or SAR Report. Personally, I prefer submitting the SAR because the 1099 has more personal information than you might not want to share.

◆ Social Security Number

Recent provisions in the law have changed the rules for assigning a social security number and issuing a Social Security card. Please check *www.socialsecurity.gov* for current information.

Guard your social security number when applying for scholarships — use ONLY the last four digits.

◆ Birth Certificate

If you need a copy of your birth certificate, you can go to *www.vitalrec.com*. Then you will contact the VITAL RECORDS office of the state where you were born.

You can also contact Birth Certificates USA at (800)315-7678 for assistance. (They charge about $56.00 for the search.) If you were born at home, you might try calling the City Hall in the city or town where you were born.

◆ Letters of Recommendation

Many applications request three letters written by a professor, teacher, principal, counselor, employer or any professional who knows you well and is willing to write a support letter on your behalf.

◆ Photocopy of Driver's License or Photo Identification

You will need a color copy of your driver's license. Copy shops may tell you that they can legally only make an enlarged copy or they may advise you to make your own color copy. (If you have ever made a black and white photocopy, you will understand the necessity for color.)

◆ Photocopy of Alien Registration or Naturalization Papers

Same as the above directions.

◆ Photo

On rare occasions, you may be asked for a head shot photo, but in the last twelve years, I have only seen one request for a photo.

Although I suggest that students keep all of their information in their three ring portfolio, it might be safer to make copies of your driver's license, social security number, birth certificate, alien registration or naturalization papers, and W-2 forms and file the information in a safe place at home. In your portfolio, you might write a reminder of the safe place that you have selected — you will want your personal information to remain confidential. There are far too many stolen identities — it is best to be extremely cautious.

Checklist

☐ Several copies of official transcripts and several unofficial

☐ SAT scores

☐ W-2 Forms, 1099

☐ SAR Report

☐ Social Security Number

☐ Driver's license or photo identification

☐ Alien registration or naturalization papers

☐ Copy of current photo

Creating Your Portfolio

One of the major tenets of **The Andrews System** is the creation of an organized portfolio of all the necessary documents needed to apply for any scholarship or grant. The more organized you are the faster you can turn an application around. Everything at your fingertips.

First, you will need a three inch **extended** D-ring binder, page dividers (alphabet, months, blanks to custom label), plastic sheet protectors that open at the top.

Other necessary supplies include 8 ½ x 11 paper (20 pound weight), legal-size envelopes, organization sheets (sample at the end of this chapter), a roll of forever postage stamps, and three pens (black, red and green). For the applications that are mailed in, you will need twelve white large envelopes (9 x 12). This size is important in order to send all documents unfolded.

Included at the back of this chapter is a copy of a status sheet. Instruction will be given later explaining the function of a status sheet. A supply of a dozen status sheets should be enough to get you started. Try not to cut corners by eliminating this step. Organization is very essential to meeting deadlines and remaining in control of the application process.

Note
*Don't forget to download the forms and spreadsheets available on the website **www. findingmoneyforcollege.com**.*

Your goal is to find and apply for at least one hundred scholarships for which you qualify. With that many possibilities, you must develop good time management and organization skills in order maintain control of the process. It is very easy to miss deadlines if you are not diligent in maintaining your portfolio.

◆ Deadlines and Instructions

I can't emphasize enough the importance of following the directions and making your deadlines. Let's face it the job of the person deciding who gets the scholarship is tough enough.

ANY excuse to disqualify an applicant makes their job easier. Sloppy and incomplete forms, applications that show up after the due date, and bang right into the wastebasket. Doing a pretty good job or getting most of it done just isn't going to cut it. So good organizational skills are a must for this system to work.

That said, if you're not super organized, **DON'T WORRY!! YOU'RE IN GOOD HANDS.** I've done all the organizing for you! You just have to follow my specific directions and you will turn in mistake-free applications.

Checklist

- ☐ Three-inch **extended*** D-ring binder (* A regular width binder will hide the labels.)

- ☐ Organizer Sheets #1 to #4

- ☐ A–Z page dividers

- ☐ January–December page dividers

- ☐ Eight extended dividers to custom label

- ☐ Plastic sheet protectors that open on top

- ☐ 8 ½ x 11 white paper (20 pound weight)

- ☐ Envelopes — legal size (12 to start)

- ☐ Roll of Forever postage stamps

- ☐ Black pen

- ☐ Red pen

- ☐ Green pen

- ☐ Large white envelopes 9 x 12

- ☐ Status Sheets

Assembling Your Portfolio

Use the checklist that is included on the previous page and purchase all of the materials necessary to set up your three-ring extended binder. You can try places like Walmart and Target to purchase your binder, dividers, sheet protectors, 8 ½ x 11 paper, legal-size envelopes, 9 x 12 white envelopes, and some good writing pens. Having a black pen is important since some applications specify that the forms must be completed in black ink. A red and green pen is necessary to keep your calendars updated with deadlines.

Note
A good black pen is a must for filling out documents.
Many documents get scanned or copied before being judged. A clear and neat copy is easier to read and enhances your eligibility.

Once you have purchased all of your materials and supplies and made copies of organizer sheets, status sheets, and printed out your calendar, assemble your portfolio in the following sequence:

1. Organizer Sheets #1–#4 (see Appendix)

2. January–December Dividers & Printed Calendar Sheets*

3. A–Z Dividers

4. Eight Extended Page Dividers

5. Several sheet protectors behind each blank divider

6. Status Sheets

You will need to make labels for your set of blank dividers. I prefer to use labels by Avery — the computer-generated labels are professional looking. If set up properly, this portfolio will serve you well for searching grants and scholarships through graduate school.

*Many computer programs have downloadable calendars. Use the style that offers the largest spaces for recording your deadlines and mailing dates.

The following are the titles for the blank labels:

1. **Documents**

   Alien Registration*

   Birth Certificate*

   Driver's License*

   Photo

   SAT Scores

   Social Security Card*

   Transcripts

   W-2 Forms, 1099*

2. **Guidelines for Letter of Recommendation**

3. **FAFSA Application and SAR Report**

4. **Letters**

   Letters of Recommendation

   Request for Letter of Recommendation

   Thank You for Letter of Recommendation

   Thank You for Scholarship

5. **Personal Data Form**

6. **Personal Statements**

7. Résumés

8. Status Sheets

*Be sure to keep these in a safe place. Under the divider, you can make a note to yourself on the location of the "safe place".

Note

The labels can be downloaded from www.findingmoneyforcollege.com. The dividers that you purchase for your binder come with printable labels. The template on my website is aligned to fit the labels.

Section 2
Writing to Win

The Personal Statement

Preparation for Writing Your Personal Statement

What They Want

Samples of Beginning Paragraphs

Samples of Personal Essays

Letters

Scholarship Résumé

Notes

The Personal Statement

Your personal statement is one of the most important parts of your scholarship application. There is a reason that we say, "I won a scholarship". It is a competition. This section of the book will provide tips on how to write the materials that can move your application from the middle to the top of the stack.

Note

Keep reminding yourself that you are the applicant
who should be selected — it is your job to convince the judges
that you are the best candidate.

A common mistake that students make is to wait until the last minute to start writing a personal statement. By doing this, you're bound to end up with a weak statement that could negatively affect your eligibility.

Remember, you are competing with many top students who have the same or better qualifications. Your personal statement could be the deciding factor with the judges. Your statement is your opportunity to stand out as an individual. The application form shows factual information, but your personal statement paints a picture of you.

Just imagine for a moment how boring it must be to read one personal statement after another that reads like a shopping list. Instead of simply listing the honors, awards or achievements that you included on your application, include brief descriptions of your specific achievements. Keep that in mind, and the results will allow the scholarship committee to know you as the deserving candidate that you are.

Please resist the temptation to begin with: "Hello, my name is. ..." You have already written your name on the application, and all of your documents will have your name on the upper right hand corner. You want your statement to be read — a weak introduction is a sure way to have your packet end up in the reject pile.

Get those creative juices flowing and make that first paragraph compelling. You want to attract the reader's attention and entice him to keep reading. You are attempting to project an image of an interesting person who is worthy of the grant or scholarship being awarded.

Prior to writing your first draft, do some brainstorming. Sit down with a blank piece of paper and jot down the names of people or books that inspired you. Mention early influences that led you to your goal. Give some thought to significant events in your life and what you have learned about yourself through these events. Are there beliefs or causes for which you have a passion? Where do you expect to be in five or ten years and what do you envision yourself doing? Be specific in your writing — include details and interesting stories.

Once you start writing keep the focus on yourself. It's best not to include long narrative passages describing other people. You are marketing your accomplishments as a dedicated student who is committed to pursuing an education. Without using a lot of fluff or overly boasting about yourself, project a positive image of a serious student.

The average personal statement is about 500 hundred words long — that is approximately two typewritten pages double-spaced. As you think about the major influences in your life and what you have learned about yourself, consider three questions: Who am I? How did I get that way? Where am I going?

Another important point to remember is having knowledge of your chosen major and/or career. If you know the profession you want to go into, explain how your volunteer work or internship will prepare you for that field.

Note
Know something about the organization offering the scholarship.
Be curious enough to want to know why they are willing to give thousands
of dollars to students. What will make them proud to select you?

Once you've identified your long-range goals and selected a few themes from your brainstorming session, start writing your first draft. Your first writing session is just that — a draft. A strong personal statement is the result of a great deal of editing and rewriting.

Initially, write what comes to mind and be prepared to put the draft aside for a day or two. Your ultimate goal is to have approximately two pages of a well-written reflection of who you are and what you are trying to achieve.

Bear in mind that one personal statement may not be adequate for all applications. Your first one should be general, but you may be required to address a particular subject. If your ethnicity plays into the requirements for the scholarship you will need a personal statement that reflects that requirement.

Your personal statement is a very, very important document. Allow plenty of time to write and rewrite and rewrite. Make your personal statement easy to read and show that you've taken time to make it interesting. Please use spell check and proofread for missing words, typos, and repeated words. Find somebody you trust to help. Professors and counselors can also help you to refine your writing so that you have a polished and impressive personal statement.

Note
Use spell-check!
Proofread for missing words, typos, and repeats!
Rewrite, Rewrite, Rewrite!

If you are still having trouble writing your personal statement there are some terrific books out there to help you...

Money-Winning Scholarship Essays and Interviews:
Insider Strategies from Judges and Winners
by Gen and Kelly Tanabe

Ca\$h for College's Write it Right
by Cynthia Ruiz McKee and Phillip C. McKee Jr.

You might seriously consider purchasing the **McKee book.** It takes you through the whole process of writing your personal essay. In addition, there are many samples of personal statements and examples of rewrites. Since you will have to write many papers if you are pursuing a college degree, it would be a good resource to have on your shelf.

Preparation for Writing Your Personal Statement

Use these questions to jumpstart the writing process. Initially, you need to brainstorm. Once you have completed this exercise, you can decide on your basic theme. Try to stay focused — it is best to elaborate on one or two topics. **Remember!** The judges want to know who you are and which educational path you have chosen. Keep reminding yourself that YOU are the one that should receive the award. It is your job to convince them through your personal statement that you are a GREAT INVESTMENT! Believe that the scholarship is already yours, really want it, but write an essay that will make the scholarship committee take notice!

I.   If you are an immigrant or first generation American.

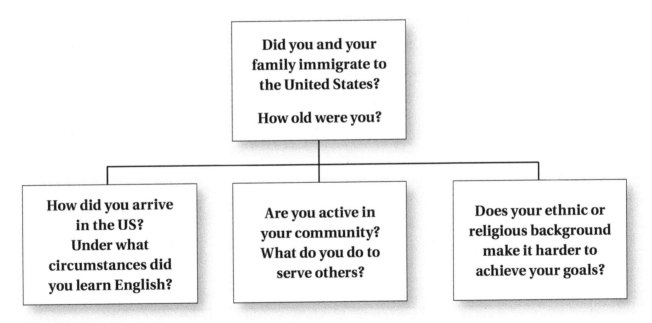

II. If you have financial hardship.

III. If you have a significant achievement.

IV. If you have a disability.

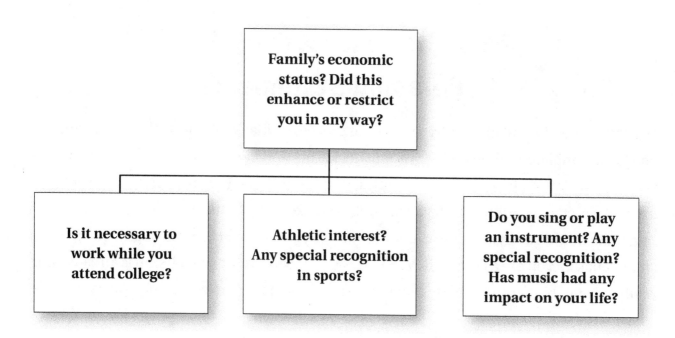

This is the time to be proud of your accomplishments. Talk about your special talents with pride and enthusiasm. If you don't tell the scholarship committee, who will? Now, there is a balance between describing your positive attributes with candor and sincerity and being pompous. Being a braggart, is not going to cut it, but, come on, you MUST let them know that you are the one that they should select.

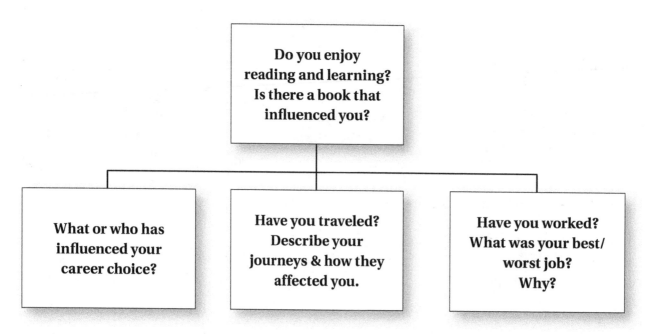

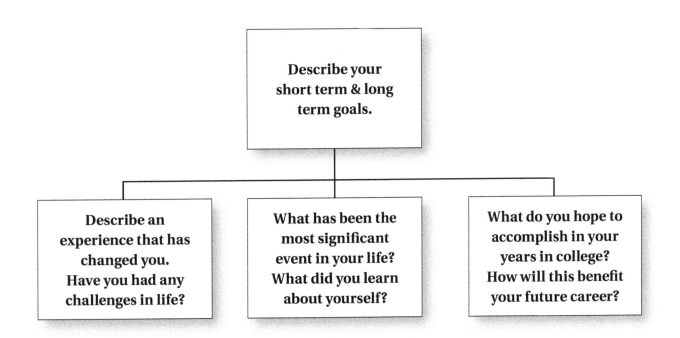

Are you getting the idea of what should be included in your personal statement? **Good!!** Most of my students had to be coaxed to start saying positive things about themselves so, you are not alone. The point is that scholarships are awarded to winners. You **must** write like a winner. Check the following page for what they want.

What They Want

Of course, it goes without saying, that the presentation of your whole scholarship packet is **critical.** It would be so sad to have all of your work discarded because the following was overlooked:

Correct Spelling — check and double check your spelling.

Good Grammar — run your grammar check on your computer.

Proper Format & Neatness — pristine, polished & professional.

Samples of Beginning Paragraphs

◆ Sample #1

When I entered college as an adult with two grown children, I was ready for a new beginning. The realization that I no longer had someone to provide me with a comfortable lifestyle was the necessary catalyst to reinvent myself. It was *sink* or swim and I was determined to not only learn to swim but also to become an excellent swimmer.

That was the starting point of my quest for knowledge. Earning a college degree became my main focus. It was all that occupied my thoughts. My first goal was to earn an associate's degree. Once I realized that I had the ability to excel as a student, I was more motivated than ever. There was no stopping me. A formal education was my path to independence.

◆ Sample #2

While in high school, I was an average student. It seems that life was a day-to-day experience and I accepted whatever came my way. To my knowledge, there were no compelling aspirations and few, if any, goals to achieve. Without a role model, a college education was not on my radar screen.

To my good fortune, I was surrounded by achievers and had a counselor who recognized potential in me. Through my mentor/advisor, I slowly understood the necessity of a formal education. Knowledge was the key to a successful life and personal fulfillment. That spark ignited a fire that is now propelling me. Now, I have a dream and that is how it all begins.

◆ Sample #3

Life for me hasn't always been moonlight and roses. At the young age of sixteen, I started living on my own. I was working in a candy store on the outskirts of San Francisco and sleeping in the home of Petra Andersson, an eighty-year-old woman that I walked home from the train station all those years ago. She was too old to be walking alone in a bad neighborhood and to show me her gratitude, she gave me shelter in her home.

With a stable place to live, I continued attending school and working at the candy store. With time, my work advanced from McDonald's to Macy's. In 2005 I took a bold step and moved to Oregon and earned a GED. The next step was to become a Certified Dental Assistant and I continued in the field for twenty years. Now the time has come to gain more education. With my new found confidence, I know that I have the necessary determination to reach my goals.

◆ Sample #4

Having been born of poor and humble beginnings, I have always had very little. My father and I were estranged from the rest of the family and struggled financially. Life continued on a downward spiral to the point of having to sell all of our family possessions. Homelessness became inevitable and, to this day, my home is my van.

For two years I worked the streets of Los Angeles as an armed security guard. The location was dangerous and each day I risked my life. To say the least, it was the source of fear and great stress. Not happy times, but I was in survival mode. Survive I did and learned some very valuable lessons; lessons which instilled wisdom in me and a great determination to succeed. A formal education is now my goal.

◆ Sample #5

My life has not been one of great want. I have never known real hunger. I have never wondered where I would rest at night, nor have I feared whether my resting place would be safe. What I have had all my life is a heart for those who have suffered greatly and a desire to help them. As a younger person, I believed that the best I could do would be to share a few dollars. I felt as though I was doing something. As I grew in age, and a little in wisdom, I started to realize that the problems are so much deeper than what a few dollars can remedy. Poverty, I have learned, is an economic, a medical, an emotional, and humanitarian problem. I wish I had a solution. I now know what I, as one person, can do. I learned it from Alicia.

◆ Sample #6

My educational goals stem from my experiences while living at Lummi Reservation in Northern Washington. It was my involvement with the lineal descendants of Chief Seattle that gave me the passion to study sociocultural anthropology. My living in a dirt poor house for eight years without heat was the most meaningful thing I have ever done. Although I didn't deliberately choose to live outside of my culture, but like Thoreau, I always believed in the natural order. There were times when we were cold and went hungry, but I walked away that much stronger from the experience.

◆ Sample #7

My years of abandonment started when my hero, my father, died at the age of thirty–eight. My world was shattered. As the baby of the family, there was no doubt that I was his favorite. He took me everywhere he went and even the most mundane activity was a treat for me. My memories are of trips to the dump and cleaning sewers. The best part about them was the ultimate stop at the tavern where I was given a soda, bag of chips, and a dime to play the juke box or play pool.

◆ Sample #8

From birth, the odds were stacked against me. Both my mother and father were heroin addicts which created an environment of domestic violence and poverty. As a child, I was so neglected that it burned a fire of determination in my soul. I was not going to subject any future child of mine to such a dark, grim lifestyle. To this day, I have a vivid memory of my father holding me up high, kissing me, and telling me he loved me. That was the last time I saw him. Days later, he was found dead in an abandoned car — he had died of an overdose.

◆ Sample #9

As a sophomore at Palm Springs High School, I had the good fortune of being part of the Health Academy which was a new program at the school. It was the greatest choice that I have ever made. It opened the door to my future career and I learned useful information about the medical field. We were not only taught how to take vital signs, but we also learned CPR and First Aid as well as basic emergency procedures. I had finally found something which totally interested me and I was so motivated that my grade point average actually went up. I was doing something that I really liked — I now had my career path and I was happy.

◆ Sample #10

From the most arduous and painful of life's experiences, come the strength, fortitude, and ability to help others through their own trials and turmoil; to know misery is to find opportunities to sow kindness. This was the lesson imparted to me long ago, not by lecture or counsel, but by the life and actions of my former neighbor — Mr. Tran. I met Mr. Tran about twelve years ago, when my family and I relocated to a small neighborhood. Our profile mirrored that of most of the other families in the neighborhood — low income and predominantly Hispanic. This made Mr. Tran, an elderly man of Asian descent, stand out even more to me. As I became acquainted with him and his involvement with the community, I learned that Mr. Tran distributed free school materials to the community at the beginning of each school year.

Remember: You must grab the reader's attention in the first paragraph. You need a "hook." Make it interesting for the judges to read.

Samples of Personal Essays

◆ Sample #1 – Alicia Eve Cunha

It has taken many years for me to truly appreciate the uniqueness of being the first generation born in the United States. As a child, I felt embarrassed that we spoke a different language, and that we didn't have running hot water. For many years a bath was a weekly event that involved carrying buckets of boiling hot water to the second-floor bathroom. For the most part, I wasn't fully aware that we were poor — I slept in a clean, dry environment and my stomach was always full, but we were, in fact, socially deprived.

Both of my parents were born and raised in the Azores Islands and immigrated to the United States as young adults. As a seventeen year old, my mother met and married my father who was a widower with four young children — he was nineteen years her senior. Together they had four children doubling the mouths that had to be fed.

Being the baby of the family meant hand-me-downs, but on the positive side there were so many people to watch over me and I was showered with love and attention. As the youngest, I was the first in the family to complete high school, and for many years that is where my education stopped. As an adult I went to community college and became a Certified Dental Assistant, got married, and had a family of my own.

Throughout the years I pursued many careers with a scattering of classes at a community college. After a number of successful jobs and what seemed to be a successful marriage, my happy days came to a screeching halt. My husband of nearly thirty years decided to change my status — I was no longer a Mrs. nor a Miss, but a dismissed. It was at that stage in my life when I realized I was a survivor. I grieved for a couple of years before deciding to return to college for a formal education.

My initial goal was very simple. I would take a computer class and another in medical terminology and believed that it would prepare me to get a job at the local hospital. I was struggling financially and had very little confidence in my ability to be a successful student. Little did I know at that stage of my life that I needed more than survival to be happy.

But, a greater power was guiding me. I met two wonderful counselors at a community college who encouraged me to at least get a two-year degree in liberal arts. I listened to their advice and soon found myself on an incredible journey. As I continued to ace most of my classes, my confidence started to soar. What a power trip that was!

That brings me to the present. I have been accepted at San Francisco State University where I will complete my undergraduate studies. After that, I will apply to graduate school to do a master of science degree in counseling. I love being on a college campus and I realize that I have an inborn talent for motivating others.

It is such a relief to finally know with certainty which career path I need to follow. There is no stopping me and I will do whatever it takes to complete my education. Every day I visualize myself in my cap and gown walking across the stage to receive my graduate degree.

◆ Sample #2 – Mary Ellen Melrose

As a teenager, I abused my body, my mind, and my spirit through a rough phase of eating disorders. I would binge eat, try quick and easy diets, and even starve myself in order to achieve what I felt was the perfect body. Like many people, I was uneducated about proper nutrition and the effects food has on your whole life. I always felt tired, cranky, insecure, unhappy, and unmotivated until I completely transformed my life.

Ironically, I owe my addiction of self-destructive habits to my present healthy lifestyle. Admittedly, my bad habits were prevalent in my life until I found confidence, determination, and ambition through healthier habits. Most importantly, providing my body with nutritious foods helped to evolve my thinking patterns. First, eating healthier provided my body with a source of energy and optimism that inspired me to become more physically active. As a result of eating healthier and working out, I developed a thirst for knowledge; so much so that I decided to attend college to pursue a career in Nutrition.

I am so eager to work in a field that helps people reach their maximum potential in life through changing their lifestyles. I have already started my journey by working part-time as a server at a health food restaurant. In addition, I started my own side business of meal prepping for my clients. For example, I cater to people who are gluten free, vegetarians, vegans, paleo, and/ or people who just want to eat healthy. I prepare meals that provide the necessary nutrients needed to sustain optimal health. My favorite part of this job is hearing my clients express how much happier, healthier, and energetic they feel.

By graduating with a degree in Nutrition, I will be able to fulfill my destiny of helping others and to motivate others to follow my lead.

◆ Sample #3 – Sophia Lynn Monroe

As far as I can remember, I have had a great love for animals and with that came a great compassion for caring for their needs. It didn't matter whether the animal was a family pet, a part of a farm, or one I encountered in the wild. As young as a six year old, I felt no fear. Seeing an injured animal or one that was in a dangerous situation brought me great sadness. Without stopping to think of my safety, I once rescued a young bull whose horns were entangled in a wire fence. The only fear that I experienced was the bull's potential injury. He needed immediate help and I was the only one available.

As you can imagine, my naïve fearlessness created great anxiety for my grandfather. It was he who felt great concern for my well-being. I made no distinction between a gentle kitten and a poisonous snake. My deep concern for the well-being of all animals is a continuing force in my life. The inevitable course for me is to enroll in the prerequisite classes which will ultimately prepare me to enter a College of Veterinary Medicine.

I understand the rigorous courses which will be required of me. Having graduated from Indio High School in the top 5 percent of my class, and completed 305 credits rather than the minimum of 220 credits, convinces me that I am sufficiently capable of reaching my dream. Not only am I fiercely determined, but I also have a burning passion to spend my life caring for these wonderful, helpless creatures. They have the ability to feel and their bodies can experience pain.

Going back to my days in middle school, I joined an after-school club with other young people who shared my interest in animals. The club turned into a class where we learned about the preparation for becoming Doctor of Veterinary Medicine and the necessary requirements for qualifying. The information I learned reinforced my decision and since then I have felt compelled to continue to follow my purpose in life.

Prior to my graduation from high school, I received a number of offers from colleges inviting me to register at their institution. The availability of scholarships forced me to really examine the benefits of graduating debt-free, but the bottom line was that I was not interested in the majors which were available to me. I couldn't put aside my love of working with animals. I must follow my dream of being a veterinarian. I feel strongly that it is my purpose in life.

Presently, I am enrolled in a scholarship class in which I am learning how to submit winning applications. It has given me the necessary hope that my graduate degree may be reached sooner rather than later. I appreciate the opportunity for being considered a candidate for the award which you are offering. However, I realize that I must work as though everything depends on me to graduate without the burden of student loans.

◆ Sample #4 – Natalie Ann Martin

There I was pregnant with my first child, scared to my core, and lacking direction in my life. Becoming a mother lit a fire in my soul and I channeled all my energy into our future. The book, *Your Best Life Now*, played a huge role in my decision to return to school shortly after my daughter came into the world. This book opened my mind to seeing that I was not living my life to my full potential. It wasn't until I dove head first into my academics that I found my purpose and zest for life. I didn't chose mathematics, math chose me. Professors helped me see that I have a gift and it should not go unanswered. Watching my dad's dedication to his work in the construction field, and how he truly loved waking up each day to go to his job, motivated me to pursue a career as a civil engineer in the construction industry.

I am eager to build schools to further the education of future generations and to construct airports for world travel and towers for communication. I want to develop places of business to boost our economy and encourage families like mine. I have learned there are ways to build with the environment in mind. I plan to implement those ideas into my daily work and developments as I recognize the earth is precious. I feel that my potential is limitless because I will work hard, achieve, and overcome.

As a result of my future successes, I see my young family thriving. We would travel the world, meet people of various cultures, and enjoy destinations that take our breath away. To experience these beautiful people, places, and animals in person would be majestic. I feel one's understanding of the universe goes only as far as you travel and experience. Tolerance is learned through encounters not inherited in your hometown. The world needs more people who are travelers and exemplify compassion, education, and tolerance. I would be able to provide for my family and for myself a life of peace, comfort, and most of all, adventure.

As a woman in a STEM major, I see myself inspiring young women (including my daughter) to go after whatever it is that makes them happy; even if the status-quo says to do the opposite. I am a young, dedicated mother, full-time student, and outdoor enthusiast devoted to a dream so big it scares me. As a first-generation college student and Coachella Valley native I am on the path to attend California Polytechnic University of Pomona (Cal Poly) in 2018. With the help of scholarships, I would be able to move my family closer to Cal Poly's undergraduate civil engineering program, purchase materials necessary to be successful, and provide childcare for my daughter while I am at school. I have found my direction, my purpose, and I am chasing after it with all my might.

Make your personal statement shine!!!

Checklist for Writing Your Personal Statement

☐ Read the guidelines for writing the personal statement that are in the application packet. Underline important words or statements.

☐ Brainstorm ideas for general topics and requirements of specific scholarships.

☐ Become informed about the organization offering the scholarship.

☐ Be clear about your career goals.

☐ Do research on prospective colleges.

☐ Know your educational plans.

☐ Start writing your first draft immediately.

☐ Put it aside for a day or two and then concentrate on editing and rewriting.

☐ Keep all drafts and notes together in a folder so you can easily revise and add.

☐ Include favorite quotations, metaphors, or analogies.

☐ Use your imagination.

☐ Once you have a reasonably good beginning, have an instructor, counselor, tutor or a trusted friend critique your writing.

☐ Make changes and reprint.

☐ Show the draft to an instructor, counselor, tutor or trusted friend as many times as necessary.

☐ Make changes and reprint.

☐ Proofread your final draft. Use spell check on your computer.

☐ Check for grammatical errors. Reprint.

☐ Make a half a dozen good quality copies — either extra copies from your computer or a professional looking photocopy from a print shop. White paper is always safe. Use at least 20-weight paper.

☐ File in your portfolio in preparation for mailing an application.

☐ Reread before mailing your application to be sure that it follows all the specific guidelines.

☐ Be sure that your name and the last four digits of your social security number are on the upper right of the page.

Dos and Don'ts of Writing Personal Essay

Dos Checklist

☐ **Do** be honest, be genuine, be you!

☐ **Do** take plenty of time for brainstorming and self-reflection to come up with unique, insightful essay ideas.

☐ **Do** ask your family, friends, mentors, and anyone else who knows you well to suggest ideas or qualities you may want to incorporate in your essay.

☐ **Do** give yourself some time, at least an hour or two, between when you write and review your finished essay.

☐ **Do** read and reread your essay, and carefully review it for errors or confusing passages.

Don'ts Checklist

☐ **Don't** lie, plagiarize, recycle a school assignment, or ask someone else to write your essay for you. (Scholarship judges really can tell).

☐ **Don't** ignore word counts or page length requirements, and don't fiddle with the font sizes or page margins to do so.

☐ **Don't** use emoticons, text message speak, or otherwise highly informal language (conversational is okay).

☐ **Don't** use your essay to praise the college you're applying to or criticize other schools, including your high school.

☐ **Don't** let yourself get stressed out. The application essay is your chance to talk about what makes you special — enjoy it!

Letters

Although many of the organizations offering scholarships provide an online application process, others still use paper and pencil versions. In order to complete a hard copy, you must write a letter requesting the application form and relevant materials. In addition, there will be other letters needed to generate references, and for every recommendation, a thank you is required. It is important to have a sample copy of each of these letters ready to personalize in your binder.

◆ Letter One — Request for an Application and Materials

This letter can be short and to the point. Remember that the person at the receiving end is busy and doesn't have time to read an essay. You are requesting an application and the requirements for qualifying — keep your words simple and direct. My preference is to use only the necessary words, but should you find the need to write more, I have included a sample with more verbiage.

◆ Letter Two — Request for a Letter of Recommendation

Most applications will require references from someone who knows you. I'm sure that family and friends who love you would be willing to write a glowing letter about your superlative qualities, but it would be best to have three letters in your binder from professionals, a counselor, professor and/or an employer who know you as a student or a diligent employee. Ideally, you would have a reference from one or two people in academics and the third from the business world.

Remember that counselors and professors receive many similar requests from other hopeful applicants. As a courtesy, ask if he or she would feel comfortable writing a positive reference on your behalf. If you receive an enthusiastic response, put your request in writing. In addition to your letter of request, include a copy of your unofficial transcripts and your personal statement. This will make it easier for your counselor or professor to write convincingly that he knows you and finds you deserving of a financial award.

Checklist for a Request for a Reference:

☐ Allow enough time for your letter of recommendation to be written.

☐ Give the writer a deadline.

☐ Include a copy of your transcripts and personal statement.

☐ For a specific scholarship, include a copy of the requirements.

☐ It might help to call or e-mail the counselor or professor after a week as a reminder.

☐ Once you receive your letter of recommendation, respond with a written thank you.

☐ THIS IS VERY IMPORTANT!! It is not only the courteous thing to do, but you may need a follow up letter.

☐ Ask permission to duplicate the letter for future applications.

☐ Duplicate the letter and have a half dozen copies ready.

◆ Letter Three — Thank You for the Letter of Recommendation

Please, please, remember that writing a thank you letter is VERY IMPORTANT. Not only is it important to write a thank you letter, but also to respond immediately. A written note would suffice, but why not keep the whole process professional? It wouldn't hurt to include a packet of decorative post-its, a nice bookmark or even a candy bar that would fit into the envelope. Let it be known that you are appreciative and aware of the niceties of life.

The following samples can be adapted to suit your personal needs:

Request for An Application
Sample One

November 19, 2019

Andrews Scholarship Fund
727 Opportunity Lane
Success, CA 92270

Attention: Eve-Marie Andrews

Dear Ms. Andrews:

Please send me an application and relevant materials for the scholarship that you are offering. I am enclosing a self-addressed stamped envelope for your convenience.

Sincerely,

Mary Antonia DaLuz

Mary Antonia DaLuz
1987 August Drive
Martinez, CA 91234
(760) 772-3960
madaluz@aol.com

Request for an Application
Sample Two

November 19, 2019

Sally Ann Jones
330 Utah Street
San Francisco, CA 95601
(650) 558-2403
SallyAnn@dc.rr.com

Scholarship Coordinator (type name if known)
David A. Cunha Liberal Studies Scholarship
9260 Third Avenue, Suite #2
San Francisco, CA 95601

Dear Scholarship Coordinator (type name if known):

I am interested in learning more about your scholarship for liberal studies majors. As a potential candidate, I would greatly appreciate any application materials or information you could send to me at this time.

Thank you for your attention to my request and for promptly forwarding the necessary materials. Earning the David A. Cunha Liberal Studies Scholarship would be an honor and would greatly assist my efforts to pursue my academic goals.

Sincerely,

Sally Ann Jones

Encl: Self addressed, stamped envelope

Financial Aid Question on the Personal Data Form

Whether you have a family that is financially able to pay for your college education or your family is living paycheck to paycheck, everyone needs scholarships for one reason or the other. There are scholarships for financial need and others are based on merit. The point is that when you are completing the Financial Need section of your Personal Data Sheet, it is not sufficient to write that you need money for college. It is a given that students need all of the financial assistance that they can get.

It is critical to maintain your dignity and to not sound as though you are begging. A "sob story" is not the way to present your case. Your words must sound professional. You can make your status known with a well-written essay. If you write your story from the heart and show enthusiasm and passion for your future career, the judges will get the message.

It is important to state that you are committed to getting your college degree no matter what you are experiencing in life. Think back to the two paragraphs that you wrote on deserving to be a winner. It is your job to convince the judges that you are the most deserving candidate. You must show that you are seeking a four, six, or maybe more years of formal education or training in order to be a contributing member of society. Yes, the right career may provide you and your family with a very comfortable lifestyle, but when an organization awards a student a $10,000 scholarship, they want it to be a good investment. Making one individual happy is not their primary mission.

Some phrases to avoid:

1. I deserve to receive a scholarship because my family is struggling.

2. I need money for my college degree.

3. Without your scholarship, I can't complete my education.

4. Although my family does not have the means, I should not be denied the opportunity to attend Harvard College.

5. All students have the right to a free education.

Please Read

Guidelines for Writing a Letter of Recommendation

As a courtesy, decline writing a letter of recommendation if you do not feel comfortable making really positive comments. Your letter may determine the award of money necessary for the student's education. If the deadline does not fit into your schedule, refer the student to someone else.

1. Introduce yourself and describe your qualifications to assess the applicant.

2. Explain how you know the applicant, for how long, and under what circumstances.

3. Supply specific factual evidence that will support the conclusions that you want the reader to infer.

4. Compare the applicant to other people you have observed.

5. Try to make applicant come alive as a person by:
    a. writing in such a way that it is clear that you know the applicant; and
    b. writing so that you convey your enthusiasm about the applicant.

6. You must show that you are qualified to make judgments about the applicant, and have had the opportunity to observe the applicant both as an individual and in comparison to others that you have observed.

Please use the following letter specifications:

•   Use college or business letterhead.

•   Select *Times New Roman* or any font that is similar in simplicity.

•   12 or 14 size font is suitable.

- Keep margins and format balanced.

- Type student's name in the header in the upper right corner.

- Below the student's name, type the student's ID #.

- Type *Letter of Recommendation* on the top center of the page.

- Make copies for use with other scholarship applications.

- Please do not fold or staple.

- Return in the enclosed envelope.

The above guidelines are based on directions given by many organizations offering scholarships to students. Consistency makes the review process easier for the committees judging the hundreds of applications received. Since many qualified students are eliminated for not following directions, it is imperative that all documents submitted look neat, organized, and professional.

Thank you for taking the time to write on this student's behalf.

Eve-Marie Andrews

Request for Letter of Recommendation

November 19, 2019

Professor Thomas Martin
College of the Desert
43-500 Monterey Avenue
Palm Desert, CA 92260

Dear Professor Martin:

I am in the process of applying for scholarships for my continuing education. One of the requirements of the application process is letters of recommendation. Do you feel comfortable writing a positive recommendation on my behalf?

During the fall semester of 2018, I was a student in your Psychology class. I am including copies of my transcripts and a personal statement to refresh your memory.

Although I am committed to my academic goals, there are some financial concerns. Receiving grants and scholarships would assure my ability to remain dedicated to my studies. Having the necessary letters of support would enhance my eligibility.

Should you have any questions I can be reached by phone or e-mail. I really appreciate your willingness to write a letter of recommendation.

Thank you,

Joseph Ferreira
16 Sheridan Street
Palm Springs, CA 97861
(760) 771-0203
jferreira@aol.com

Thank You For Letter of Recommendation

November 19, 2019

Professor Thomas Martin
College of the Desert
43-500 Monterey Avenue
Palm Desert, CA 92260

Dear Professor Martin:

My sincere thanks for taking time from your busy teaching schedule to write a letter of recommendation on my behalf. I'm sure that you are inundated with many similar requests, which add greatly to your workload.

Do you have any objection to my copying the letter, and submitting it with future scholarship applications?

Again, my thanks for giving of your time.

Sincerely,

Joseph Ferreira
(760) 771-0203

Thank You for Scholarship
Sample One

November 19, 2019

Title and Name of Contact
Name of Company
Street
City, State, Zip

Dear (Name of Contact):

Being selected to receive your $3,000 scholarship was not only thrilling, but it has brought a tremendous peace of mind for the next school year. As I mentioned in the personal statement that accompanied my application, I am committed to my education, and because of that dedication have maintained a 3.78 Grade Point Average.

This fall I will be entering graduate school at San Francisco State University, and majoring in Counseling. Not only is it a career that will allow me to help others pursue their educational goals, but my maturity will also be an asset. Since I am so enthusiastic about returning to school and earning a much coveted college degree, I know that I can be an inspiration to other returning adults.

Again, my sincere thanks for being chosen as your candidate for the generous scholarship. Your vote of confidence has been very encouraging, and I will continue to give my studies my all. There is no stopping me from completing my graduate degree in two years — having financial assistance allows me to really concentrate on my educational goals.

Sincerely,

Alicia Ann Martin

Thank You for Scholarship
Sample Two

November 6, 2019

Mary Louise Benton
141 W. Third Avenue, #227
Boston, MA 94910

Cunha Family Scholarship Fund
727 Opportunity Lane
Success, CA 92270

Dear Ms. Cunha:

How thrilling it was to be selected to receive the Cunha Family Scholarship of three thousand dollars ($3,000). Since I am preparing to enter graduate school this coming fall, your support will ease the burden of tuition and the purchase of the required textbooks.

As stated in my application, I am planning to receive a master of science degree in counseling at San Francisco State University. Presently, I am completing my undergraduate studies at San Francisco State University, and have attained a grade point average of 3.87. I have been told that I will be graduating Magna Cum Laude.

Having returned to college at a mature age, I understand the challenges that reentry women face. Once I have my graduate degree, I am planning on working at a community college where I can encourage other women to follow their dreams.

My sincere thanks for selecting me, and for honoring me with your scholarship; I am committed to being a dedicated student.

Sincerely,

Mary Louise Benton

Scholarship Résumé

Earlier in this chapter, you learned about writing a personal statement — a personal statement describes who you are, in the present, and addresses your future goals. A résumé, on the other hand, lists your past accomplishments. A scholarship résumé differs in format from a job search résumé even though much of the content is the same. It is not necessary to list your work experiences in reverse chronological order, nor is it necessary to use the standard action verbs to describe your responsibilities.

The easiest way to start if you have never written a résumé is to sit in front of a blank computer or several blank pieces of paper. I like to start off with the pencil and paper version because I am visual, and can create blocks of words and use all of my colored highlighters to designate categories. You might use the following categories as a starting point:

Accomplishments/Awards/Childcare Experience/Community Service/Honors/Management Experience/Professional & Social Organizations/Special Training/Skills/Talents/Travel/ Volunteer Work/Work Experience

Have you had any extraordinary experiences such as being raised abroad; taking a seminar from a well-known personality; having your writing published; opening your own business; working on a major campaign; or even appearing on television or in a movie?

Section 3
Apply Yourself

The Right Track

Organization Checklist

Applications

Checklist for Applications

First Stop FAFSA

Checklist/Before Beginning a FAFSA

Grants and Scholarships

Surfing the Internet

Scholarship Websites

College Based Financial Assistance

E.O.P.S.

C.A.R.E. Program

College Based Scholarships

Research

47

Notes

The Right Track

I am about to REVEAL to you the key to the system, the places and methods for finding thousands of scholarships. Before I can do that there is one final piece of housekeeping. After all, if your goal is applying for 100 scholarships that's a lot of information to track. Remember, the main tenets of this system are perfect applications and no missed deadlines. So there is one organizational step remaining: Tracking.

Once you start finding scholarships, it is vital to record and file each award in a systematic manner. For three or four scholarships, it is easy to keep track of important dates. But, if you are diligent and committed to finding money for your education, the only way to be in control of your search is to record and file information immediately.

By now, your portfolio should be in order. It is important to use the following sequence of materials:

1. Organization sheets

2. January–December dividers

3. Insert your calendar sheets behind the appropriate month

4. A–Z alphabet dividers — to file suitable scholarships

5. Eight extended dividers with the following labels:

6. **Documents**

   Alien Registration*

   Birth Certificate*

   Driver's License*

   Photo

SAT Scores

Social Security Card*

Transcripts

W-2 Forms, 1099*

7. Guidelines for Letter of Recommendation

8. FAFSA Application and SAR Report

9. Letters

Letters of Recommendation

Request for Letter of Recommendation

Thank You for Letter of Recommendation

Thank You for Scholarship

10. Personal Data Form

11. Personal Statements

12. Résumés

13. Status Sheets

Procedure for Recording Scholarships

Sources of Scholarships and Grants:

Internet

Books

Counselors, Instructors, Departments

Financial Aid Office

Local Organizations

Block out times on your calendar for doing your research. When you set up your schedule, designate several hours a week for your scholarship search. Record the days and times in your calendar.

When you find scholarships on the Internet for which you qualify, print out a copy of the requirements and deadlines. At the end of the day, record each scholarship in your scholarship organizer sheet—include all of the relevant information. Find the month when the scholarship is due and with a red pen make note of the deadline. Back up 3 to 4 weeks and with a green pen, record the date when the scholarship should be mailed. File the scholarship alphabetically.

Organization Checklist

Set a time every week to complete the application process. Take the following steps:

☐ Read the directions carefully.

☐ Read the directions again.

☐ Fill out the application.

☐ Pull all of the *required* documents from your portfolio.

☐ Put all the necessary documents in the same order listed in the directions.

☐ Include **ONLY** the documents requested.

☐ Make a photocopy of all of the documents.

☐ Put all of the original documents and the completed application in the 9 x 12 envelope.

☐ Don't staple or fold anything.

☐ Complete a status sheet.

☐ Attach your status sheet to all of your photocopied documents — you need a copy of everything submitted for your records.

☐ Make proper notations on your scholarship organization sheet.

☐ File the status sheet and copies alphabetically.

☐ In pencil, write the mailing date on the envelope.

☐ Be sure you have enough postage on the envelope.

☐ Check your calendars on a weekly basis to assure that you mail applications in a timely fashion.

Applications

The opportunity to complete an application online is fast becoming the most efficient method of submitting your request for a money award. For students who do not have a computer at home, please check the local library. Many colleges provide this service for their students.

There will still be the need, with some scholarships, to write a letter requesting an application and then completing a paper and pen version. When requesting an application by mail, you need to include a self-addressed stamped envelope — a legal size (#10) envelope will suffice.

The legal size envelope necessitates folding the application, but it will need less postage. With the recent increase to fifty-five cents for Forever stamps, this may be a good way to keep your costs down.

Some organizations are more particular than others about the manner in which you submit your documents. As a general rule, I usually suggest that students be fastidious about the appearance of the application and all of the supporting materials that are included in the packet. With that in mind, I prefer sending the self-addressed envelope in the 9 x 12 size rather than the standard legal size envelope.

The goal is to present all of the documents without any creases, smudges, or penciled in corrections. The neatness and organization of your materials reveal a great deal about you. When the judges are making a decision about two equally qualified applicants, the person who has submitted an attractive and easy to read packet will be selected.

Always bear in mind that for each scholarship there are hundreds of eager candidates. The first person to handle the applications is faced with a huge stack that must be reduced to a manageable number. Many well-qualified students are eliminated because the packet is not complete and/or appears as though it has been thrown together with little thought.

Ideally, the application is completed on a computer. This will guarantee a neat and easy to read document. Many scholarships allow for online applications with the option of filling in the blanks and then submitting. On occasion, you may have to transport it to your word document and complete the form in Word.

If using a pen is your only option, black or dark blue ink is required. Buy a good pen that writes well and reserve it for the application process. Some application directions clearly state that the form be completed with black ink. **Always** follow directions.

It may seem that this is a rigid requirement, but dark ink is easier to read. In many cases applications may be scanned or photocopied to allow several judges their own copies to review — black or *dark* blue ink produces clearer copies.

When using a paper and pen application form, make a copy to use as a worksheet. Once you have answered all of the questions and completed all of the blanks, transfer all of the data to the final copy.

Whenever you have a choice, complete your application online and submit. If supplementary documentation is required, you may have to print out an application to use as a worksheet and a second copy to be used as a final copy.

Checklist for Applications

☐ Print and mail letter requesting an application and other necessary information.

☐ Purchase a good black pen and reserve it for your scholarship applications.

☐ Have available an adequate supply of 20 pound, 8 ½ x 11 paper.

☐ Buy a supply of legal size or 9 x 12 white envelopes.

☐ Purchase a roll of Forever postage stamps.

☐ Make arrangements to use library or college computers if you don't have one at home. You may have to reserve computer time. Plan ahead.

☐ Read directions carefully.

☐ Be super neat and organized.

☐ If anyone has helped you, send a note of thanks.

☐ Submit on time.

Now you're ready to start applying.
First Stop FAFSA

FAFSA
The One Financial Aid Package
Every Student Should Apply For:

www.fafsa.ed.gov/

Note

The FAFSA is the vehicle for determining whether you qualify for federal, state, and local financial assistance.
If you have not completed the FAFSA, complete it as soon as possible.

Note

At your college, the Financial Aid office has applications in either English or Spanish.

You have a choice of completing the paper version or of completing the form online. The application forms for the paper version are in the Financial Aid Office — you will find an English or Spanish version. If you decide to do the online version, my suggestion is to complete the Pre-Application Worksheet first, and then transfer the information to the actual FAFSA application. Applying online is really the **preferred method** since the accuracy rate increases significantly. You also have a faster rate of return of the SAR. Many scholarship applications request a SAR (Student Aid Report). This report summarizes the information you submit on your FAFSA. You also have the option of submitting a copy of your tax returns. Given the choice, I would feel more comfortable submitting the SAR.

The US Department of Education has posted the following benefits of using FAFSA on the Web:

- FAFSA on the Web is faster than applying for aid by paper.

- FAFSA on the Web uses skip logic based on your particular information, so you will need to answer fewer questions than on the paper application.

- FAFSA on the Web checks your answers before you submit your application, so there is less chance your application will be rejected because of missing on conflicting information.

- You can save application information so that it can be completed and transmitted at a later time.

- FAFSA on the Web can be used on Windows or Macintosh computers, using the most popular Netscape and Microsoft browser versions.

- FAFSA on the Web doesn't require software to be installed, so you can complete the application immediately.

- You can access FAFSA on the Web from anywhere, including school or home, making it more convenient to complete the application.

- FAFSA on the Web can support an unlimited number of users, allowing thousands of students to apply at once.

After processing your FAFSA, the Department of Education mails your SAR to you and sends a copy electronically to the schools you list on your FAFSA. The schools use your SAR's Expected Family Contribution (EFC) number to determine if you will receive federal financial aid. If you qualify, the school prepares a financial aid package to help you meet your financial need. Financial need is the difference between your school's cost of attendance (including living expenses), as calculated by your school, and your EFC.

Once the school has calculated your eligibility for financial aid, you will be notified by mail through an award letter, and will be advised of the date that the money will be available.

Federal Student Aid will be paid through your school. The amount of your financial aid award depends on whether:

- You're a full-time or part-time student

- You attend school for a full academic year or less

- You believe you have special circumstances such as unusual medical or dental expenses or other financial hardships

Checklist/Before Beginning a FAFSA

For the 2020–2021 school year, you will need financial information from 2019. You will need to refer to:

☐ Social Security number

☐ Driver's license (if any)

☐ Your W-2 Forms and other records of money earned

☐ Your (and your spouse's, if you are married) 2019 Federal Income Tax Return — IRS Form 1040, 1040A, 1040EZ, 1040Telefile, foreign tax return, or tax return from Puerto Rico, Guam, American Samoa, the US Virgin Islands, the Marshall Islands, the Federated States of Micronesia

☐ Your parent's 2019 Federal Income Tax Return (if you are a dependent student)

☐ Your 2019 untaxed income records — Social Security, Temporary Assistance to Needy Families, welfare, or veterans benefits records

☐ Your 2019 bank statements

☐ Your 2020 business and investment mortgage information, business and farm records, stock, bond, and other investment records

☐ Your alien registration card (if you are not a US citizen)

Once you have gathered all of the necessary documents, do the following:

☐ Complete the Pre-Application Worksheet.

☐ Plan how to sign your FAFSA.

☐ Speed the process with your PIN (sign your FAFSA electronically).

☐ Establish your eligibility — citizen, non-citizen; high school diploma or GED; states may use your FAFSA to award additional aid from their programs.

Note important deadlines.

Your form must be received no later than June 30, 2020, 8:00 P.M. Eastern Standard Time.

Colleges and states may have earlier deadlines.

2020–2021 FAFSA/Renewal on the Web: Pre-Application Worksheet

Use this worksheet to help you collect your and your parents' financial information before you begin your 2020–2021 Web application. You can obtain more detailed application information, such as how to properly complete the FAFSA, the purpose of the FAFSA questions, and how information should be reported in some unusual cases, on the Web at *http://www.ed .gov/prog_info/SFA/FAFSA/*.

Grants and Scholarships

Unlike student loans, grants and scholarships are FREE MONEY. Neither a grant nor a scholarship needs to be paid back. You need to apply for grants and scholarships and the process involves completing an application form, writing a personal statement, submitting letters of recommendation and submitting different items in the application packet. This is what you learn to do in **The Andrews System**.

The difference between a grant and a scholarship is that grants are usually given by non-profit organizations or government offices. The grant money can be used to pay for a variety of expenses such as transportation, resource materials, and sometimes even secretarial assistance.

A scholarship, on the other hand, is usually generated by a specific business, private individual, special organizations whose main money making projects support students who are in financial need and/or for a student's academic excellence. The eligibility criteria vary with each scholarship and although the application process varies to some degree for each award, **The Andrews System** prepares you for successfully applying for either grants or scholarships.

Note

In a nutshell, grants and scholarships are both FREE.
The difference is in the source and how the money is used.

◆ Examples of Grants

The following are grants that are generated through the FAFSA application (see below):

◆ Federal Pell Grant

Awarded to undergraduate students who have not earned a bachelor's or a professional degree. Eligibility is based on financial need, costs to attend college and your status as a full- or part-time student. Maximum award for 2019–2020 year is $6,195.

◆ FSEOG

Undergraduates with *exceptional* need. Pell Grant recipients with the greatest need will be considered first. You can receive $100–$4,000 a year depending on the financial aid policies at your college.

◆ Academic Competitiveness

This is in addition to the Pell Grant for first-year students who graduated after January 1, 2019. Up to $750 for 1st year of undergraduate studies and up to $1,300 for 2nd year undergraduate students.

◆ *National Science & Math* (Nat'l Smart Grant)

This is for 3rd and 4th years of undergraduate full-time students who are eligible for the Pell Grant. Students must be majoring in physical, life or computer sciences, math, technology, engineering, or in a foreign language determined critical to national security. GPA must be at least 3.0 in coursework required by major. Up to $4,000 for each of the 3rd and 4th years.

◆ Institutional Grants

Colleges provide institutional grants to help make up the difference between college costs and what a family can be expected to contribute.

Other institutional grants, known as merit awards (scholarships) are based on academic achievement.

◆ Institutional Financial Aid: Grants and Scholarships from Your . . . Studentcaffe.com Nonfederal Financial Aid Options for Students

Institutional aid is offered to **students** by the schools they plan to attend. Colleges may offer their own loans, but more often **institutional** aid is given in the form of **grants** and scholarships to **students** who either demonstrate financial need or qualify academically. This money **does not** need to repaid.

Surfing the Internet

In the last several years, there has been a rapid growth of websites offering scholarships and grants. This method of searching and applying for college money saves times and postage.

Several of the websites require that you complete a profile that includes, in addition to your name, address and e-mail: your major and/or career goals, special interests, ethnic background, and grade point average. This information is stored in their database for possible matches.

Periodically, you will receive an e-mail message notifying you of scholarships that fit your needs. At that point, you read the eligibility requirements, and you can either download the application or request more information.

Applying online is an efficient way of completing an application and submitting your personal statement. You save on postage and have the assurance of meeting application deadlines.

One of the most popular websites is *www.fastweb.com*. In addition to available scholarships and grants, you can subscribe to a free newsletter that covers issues related to finding money for college. Examples of the services offered by FASTWEB are:

Scholarships

- Top 10 Tips for Winning Scholarship Applications

- Making Sense of Scholarships

Financial Aid

- What to Do If Your Financial Aid Package Isn't Enough

- The Procrastination Guide to Financial Aid

Money/College Life

- Credit Card Selection Savvy

- Taking Time Off. Interim Programs

Career Planning

- How to Land an Internship

- Career Success Timeline

Recently, I browsed the FASTWEB website and signed in as a potential subscriber. The profile questionnaire has been expanded to include information that might be of value to FASTWEB sponsors. Many organizations will pay to have your personal information, thus allowing FASTWEB to provide many FREE valuable services to students. To a great extent the information might benefit the student, but should you want to maintain privacy, be sure to click "no thank you" when completing your profile.

As you will note on the list of scholarship websites on the next page, there are many available sources. Two of my favorites are *www.absolutelyscholarships.com* and *www.freschinfo.com*. My most recent discovery is really user friendly. Try out *www.schoolsoup.com*.

If you do not have a personal computer with Internet access, most colleges provide computers for student use. Public libraries are also a good resource.

Computer prices have become more affordable — buying one should be a priority. Being able to access money for college will ensure your being able to cut down your work hours and to devote more time to studies. In addition, you will be able to do research for all of your classes, and to turn in assignments that are neat and easy to read. Having your own computer could have a very positive effect on your grade point average — the higher your grade point average, the more opportunities for being awarded scholarship money.

Incidentally, many scholarships will allow you to use the award money to purchase a computer. You do need to follow the guidelines spelled out by the organization offering you financial assistance.

Scholarship Websites

www.schoolsoup.com — I have personally helped many students purchase books online — the used books that I have ordered have been in excellent condition.

www.chciyouth.org

2007 National Directory of Scholarships, Internships, and Fellowships for Latino Students. Click on scholarships — you will find an application. In addition, there are some Tips for Applying for Scholarships.

www.Collegexpress.com

www.scholarships.com/

"Get instant and unlimited free access to an extensive list of college scholarship and grant opportunities customized just for you."

www.fastweb.com

This scholarship site is one of the most recognized. Be sure to make it clear if you don't want your information shared with related sites. If that is your wish, you can click "no thanks".

"The most complete source of local scholarships, national scholarships and college specific scholarships. 1.3 million scholarships worth over $3 billion."

www.collegescholarships.com

"New scholarships are posted monthly. This free quality information includes all of the details you need to apply now, including eligibility requirements, deadlines, amounts…"

www.fastaid.com

"The world's largest and oldest private sector free scholarship database. 20 years of Scholarship Research. Constantly updated."

www.gocollege.com

Click Financial Aid and then click Scholarships

"Gain FREE access to over 2.4 million individual awards — that's over $3.4 billion in scholarships."

www.brokescholar.com

"The home of 650,000 scholarship award listings." Create a profile.

www.hsf.net

Several years ago all twenty of my students who applied for this scholarship, WON. The total winnings were $50,000. To qualify, you need to be at least 50% Hispanic. It is very competitive. Follow directions precisely!!!

www. Scholly.com

This site was started by a participant on Shark Tank on television. The wonderful feature is that they have a 98% rate of accuracy when it comes to matching your profile. It is very important to be as accurate as possible when submitting your goals, interests, and all personal information. (This is not a guaranty that you will win, but it means that you will more than likely fit the eligibility requirements.) There is a small monthly fee ($1.99), but it is well worth it. I highly recommend this site.

And amazingly...

www.google.com
Type in "scholarships for..."
(Anything that is unique about yourself
and/or your major.)

College Based Financial Assistance

Note

E.O.P.S. and CARE are California-based programs. If you are attending one of the 109 community colleges in California, the program is, more than likely, available to you if you meet the eligibility requirements. This is a great way to get a two year degree without taking money from your pocket. If you're not from California contact your local community college to see if there are similar programs

E.O.P.S. (Extended Opportunity Programs and Services)

The E.O.P.S. program for community colleges was established by the Legislature through Senate Bill 164. The program became effective in November, 1969. Since that time the program has grown, and through the addition of staff, has been able to increase the support services to its students.

The main focus of the program is to provide counseling services and financial assistance to students who come from low-income families. Students who are in need of improving their academic and vocational skills are encouraged to enroll in the program.

E.O.P.S. will provide qualified students with direct support services including financial aid, academic, career and personal counseling. In addition, laptop computers are available to ensure that assignments are completed legibly and easy to read. These support services will allow the student to progress beyond high school and obtain the confidence and academic and vocational skills necessary for better career employment opportunities.

EOPs Program Eligibility Requirements

Must meet all:
- Be a California Resident or AB540 Student
- Qualify for the California College Promise Grant (Formerly BOG Enrollment Fee Waiver) A or B
- Full-time enrollment — 12 units minimum
- Must have less than 70 degree units from all colleges attended (official transcripts are required).
- Be in good standing with the college you are attending.

And Meet One of the Following Criteria:
- Have not earned a high school diploma or GED
- Graduated from high school with less than a 2.5 grade point average

- Previously enrolled in remedial course work in high school or college
- Other program specific criteria
  - The student is a first generation college student (neither parent has successfully attended college); or
  - The student is a member of an underrepresented group targeted by district/college student equity goals; or
  - The primary language spoken in the student's home is/was non-English
  - The student is a current or former foster youth.

All financial aid is granted on the basis of student financial need. The amount of aid a student receives is determined from the information recorded on the financial aid forms. This form shows the difference between the student's resources and a standard yearly budget. Financial aid funds can be used to pay for fees, books, supplies, room and board, transportation and other personal expenses.

E.O.P.S. offers the following:

1. E.O.P.S. Financial Aid Grants

2. Tutoring Services

3. Career Information

4. Counseling Services

5. Fall Orientation

6. Assistance with applications, admission, registration and other college procedures

7. Peer Advising Services

8. Assistance with the transfer process to four-year universities

9. Recruitment of low income students

10. Book Grants

11. Laptop computer loans

C.A.R.E. Program

CARE (Cooperative Agencies Resources for Education) helps single parents on Public Assistance (TANF) complete a community college education — an education that will provide the opportunity for better jobs, financial self-sufficiency and independence.

Each CARE participant must be: a single parent, head of the household, a TANF recipient, at least 18 years of age, E.O.P.S. eligible, a full-time student and have at least one child under the age of 14.

The above services that are offered by E.O.P.S. are also available through CARE. In addition, food vouchers are available for the college cafeteria during class time.

College Based Scholarships

Many colleges have in-house scholarships available to their enrolled students. Most of these require that the student be enrolled in at least 12 units (full-time status) and maintain a minimum grade point average of 2.5. At some colleges, special incentive scholarships have been set up for students who are enrolled part time with a grade point average of 2.0. Be sure to check with the financial aid office at your college to become familiar with any and all money sources.

Note

College of the Desert in Palm Desert, CA is a great example of a community college that offers eighty to a hundred scholarships to their enrolled students — students receive anywhere from several hundred to several thousand dollars each year. The college is blessed with a large population of generous donors who contribute to private scholarships.

If you are attending a community college that is lacking in these resources, you might initiate some community action through your Alumni Association or through the local Chamber of Commerce. You might also start a Scholarship Club through your Student Activities office.

How about consulting with the administration to start a Scholarship class? Any college that is interested can contact me for a course outline for the Curriculum Committee's approval. I will be happy to share my class syllabus and teaching materials. My contact at the College of the Desert is *emandrews@collegeofthedesert.edu.*

Research: There are more scholarships out there.

In this book, you have been introduced to many websites and scholarship books. Although the Internet has become one of the best sources of scholarships, you need to cast a wide net in order to find the hundreds of financial awards available to students. This process takes time and perseverance even though there is a great deal of scholarship and grant money for your education.

Your main resources will be the scholarship websites, scholarship books, and college-based awards.

It is not unusual for students to find at least twenty or twenty-five scholarships for which they qualify. Without very careful organization and a system for filing and retrieving information, this process becomes overwhelming. For this reason, **setting up your portfolio is an absolute must** if you are going to submit applications in a timely fashion.

As mentioned in a previous chapter, your portfolio will contain calendars, scholarship organization forms, sections to file your scholarships alphabetically, personal statements, scholarship résumés, letters of recommendation, etc.

When you find a scholarship on the Internet, print out a copy of the eligibility requirements and all of the pertinent information necessary to apply for that particular award. Temporarily insert all of the printouts in the front pocket of your portfolio. At the end of the day or any designated time, enter the information in your scholarship organizer form at the front of the portfolio. Record the deadline on the appropriate calendar date in your portfolio, and then, back up a month and record the mailing date on your calendar.

You need to allow several weeks for the application to arrive at its destination prior to the deadline. Once all of the proper notations are made in your portfolio, file the scholarship alphabetically in your three-ring binder.

You will find that many applications can be completed online — this is a bonus since you save the step of writing to request an application. You also save postage that can quickly add up at 82¢ plus the cost of paper and envelope per application request. When you must do the paper and pen version, it is mandatory that you submit a self addressed stamped envelope (SASE). Without the SASE, you will not receive any of the necessary documents to complete the application. Be sure that you read the directions several times and follow the necessary requirements.

It is important to be mindful of the value of your time, therefore, write neatly when recording information. It is counterproductive to recopy or reprint the same process twice. Research can be a very tedious process, but the success of receiving many scholarships is based on applying for many awards, following directions, and applying in a timely fashion. Let's face it, you will not receive every scholarship for which you qualify! Receiving a half a dozen out of twenty or thirty scholarships is very possible if you qualify and submit a neat and very organized packet.

It is also a good idea to check your financial aid office for scholarships that are posted on a bulletin board and/or binder. Let instructors and counselors know that you are interested in applying for scholarships — they might have received a notice that would be of interest to you.

Section 4
Don't Fall for False Claims

Scams

Reporting Scams

Identity Theft and College Students

Notes

Scams

Sad to say, there are many individuals who do not have your best interests at heart. You are lured by guarantees of customized scholarship searches and actual financial awards. There is even an organization that will complete your FAFSA application for a preposterous fee.

A number of years ago I actually had a student in a scholarship class whose parents were ready to hand over $1,000 for "guaranteed" scholarships and being accepted into the college of the student's choice. Fortunately, the parents came in to talk to me, and I convinced them, finally, not to get involved.

This same family had relatives who, even though they work very hard for their meager incomes, fell for the promises of the scam operation. The only thing that they received for their $1,000 was a very generic list of scholarship resources. I was happy to have saved one family, but, unfortunately, several hundred thousand people a year are cheated by scholarship scams.

Do not pay any application fees, advance fees on scholarship loans or get involved with any "guaranteed" scholarship search services. I would also stay away from free seminars for financial assistance. Sometimes you gain some useful information, but these seminars are usually a front for financial aid consulting services that charge healthy fees.

The **Federal Trade Commission's** consumer alert on Scholarship Search Scams suggest looking for these six signs:

1. "This scholarship is guaranteed or your money back."

2. "You can't get this information anywhere else."

3. "May I have your credit card or bank account number to hold this scholarship for you?"

4. "We'll do all the work."

5. "The scholarship will cost some money."

6. "You've been selected by a 'national foundation' to receive a scholarship; (for just a small handling fee we can send you a check)" or "You're the finalist in a scholarship contest, (the handling fee will be …)" and you never entered that scholarship.

Reporting Scams

If you have any suspicion about a possible scam, gather all of the documents that you have and get a second opinion. The financial aid office at your college and the scholarship counselor can assist you in confirming your concerns about the legitimacy of an organization.

The following are contacts for reporting scams:

National Fraud Information Center
P.O. Box 65868
Washington, D.C. 20035
1-800-876-7060

Your state's Attorney General's Office.

Correspondence Branch
Federal Trade Commission, Room 200
6th Street and Pennsylvania Avenue, NW
Washington, D.C. 20580

Better Business Bureau
1-703-525-8277 for phone numbers of BBB
branches nationwide

If any part of the transaction took place through the mail — you should check with the US Postal Inspection Service.

Chief Postal Inspector

475 L'Enfant Plaza, SW

Room 3021

Washington, D.C. 20260-2100

1-800-654-8896

Also, please send information about any possible scam or suspicious advertisement to *www. scams@finaid.org* with the name of the company in the subject line. You may also fax FINAID at 1-412-422-6189.

If in doubt about the terms of a scholarship application, *don't* send any money. There may be a couple of instances where a very small fee is requested for an application. If it seems legitimate and you want to gamble because the award is very attractive, get a second opinion from a reliable source.

For students who are majoring in education, there are some scholarships available to student members of the California Teachers' Association. To become a member there is a fee of about $30.00. This is not a scholarship application fee, but a membership fee that gives you access to conferences, newsletters and publications. This might be worth considering for both present and future benefits.

Remember, you are trying to *win* scholarships — paying out is not necessary.

Identity Theft and College Students

You must be wondering why identity theft would be included in a book which relates to college students managing money and finding ways to pay for a college education. Most students are broke and have nothing to lose, so why be concerned? Well, think again. Recent studies indicate that eighteen-to-twenty-nine-year-olds have the most ID theft complaints.

Identity thieves are after more than a few dollars or valuable possessions. Your personal identity has more potential benefits to the criminals. By stealing your birth certificate, driver's license, and social security, credit card, and bank account numbers, a thief can have a grand time charging thousands of dollars to your accounts and divesting you of every penny that you have in your bank accounts.

Identity theft generally falls into two categories. One is the casual, one-time incident which might involve a former roommate or acquaintance using your account at a local store or accessing your online account. The second category is accomplished by professionals who have become very clever at getting hold of your personal information and using it fraudulently.

College students are at a particular risk for identity theft because their credit records are mostly blank. This creates the perfect situation for identity thieves to establish new credit. Furthermore, students receive frequent applications for credit cards and 30 percent of them throw away the applications in their original condition with all of the personal information intact. To exacerbate the situation, many students fail to review their checking and credit card balances. By ignoring their funds, students become very attractive targets.

Fortunately, many colleges are changing the practice of identifying students by their social security numbers and instead issue student identification numbers. When I was a student in the early nineties, grades were posted on the professor's office door and students were identified by their social security numbers. It didn't take much research to figure out who the student was based on his placement on the list.

Another practice which I hope is on the way out is campuses allowing banks and credit card companies to set up a table on campus grounds in order to attract applicants. Guess what? The applications require just about every piece of personal information that targets the student for identity theft. The T-shirt that you will be given might end up costing you thousands of dollars. Don't do it. A free shirt just isn't worth the risk.

Be curious about how your college or university maintains records containing your personal information. Be sure to ask your college about their data management policies and inform them if you are uncomfortable about any of their procedures which may put you and other students in a vulnerable position. Good data management includes:

(This information is excerpted from Identity Theft and College Students by Danny Lents https:// idtheftawareness.com)

Access to data is on a need-to-know basis for a limited number of authorized people with background checks revealing no criminal history.

- Records are stored in a locked container/room.
- Multiple forms of identification are required to release your information.
- Release of data is entered in a log for auditing purposes.
- Data should not be removed from the secured area on laptops, thumb drives, or any other removable storage media. The data must be encrypted if it is absolutely necessary to transport data outside of the secured environment.
- Records are completely destroyed by shredding or burning when they are no longer needed.
- Discarded computers must have data permanently erased from hard drives.
- Social security numbers are not used as student IDs.
- SSNs are not requested on forms unless absolutely required.

The following are some tips for avoiding identity theft:

1. Invest in a shredder and immediately destroy any documents that include personal information.
2. Be leery of phone solicitations or organizations pretending to be legitimate. Just do not give out any personal information on the phone unless you have initiated the phone call.
3. Do not carry your social security card in your wallet. By law, you must carry a driver's license if you operate a vehicle, but both cards spell disaster.

4. Be sure that no one is standing close behind you at an ATM machine. Cell phones now have cameras.

5. Do not leave any receipts behind you at the ATM.

6. Routinely review your checking account balance and your credit card accounts.

7. Do not buy anything on a public computer.

   - A secure URL will start with "https."

   - Do not lend anyone a credit card.

   - Avoid using campus mailboxes for outgoing mail.

   - Beware of scholarship telemarketing fraud.

   - Do not pay to submit a scholarship application.

   - Do not subscribe to anything or any services on public property.

   - Follow your gut. If something doesn't feel right, say no or hang up.

Should you become a victim:

(The following information is distributed by the Office of Inspector General.)

Contact the fraud departments of the three major credit bureaus.

Equifax: www.equifax.com Phone: 1-800-685-111

   Write: P.O. Box 740241, Atlanta, GA 30374-0241

Experian: www.experian.com Phone: 1-888-397-3742

   Write: P.O. Box 9532, Allen, TX 75013

Transunion: www.transunion.com Phone: 1-800-680-7289

   Write: Fraud Victim Assistance Division,

   P.O. Box 6790, Fullerton, CA 92834-6790.

Close the accounts that you know or believe have been tampered with or opened fraudulently.

File a police report with your local police or the police in the community where the theft took place.

If you become a victim of identity theft involving federal education funds or suspect that your student information has been stolen, contact:

U.S. Department of Education, Office of Inspector General Hotline: email oig.hotline@ed.gov, 1-800-647-8733 (1-800-MISUSED) For more information, or to report an identity theft that does not involve federal education funds, visit the following sites:

- Federal Trade Commission, 1-877-IDTHEFT (1-877-438-4338)

- Internal Revenue Service, www.irs.gov

- Social Security Administration, 1-800-269-0271

- National White Collar Crime Center, http://www.nw3c.org

- Identity Theft is a Crime: Resources from the Government www.justice.gov/criminal/fraud and www.businessidtheft.org/resources/federal

No one, including students, is immune from being a potential victim of identity theft. The financial and emotional consequences of this crime are long-term and long-lasting. The information provided above gives you a number of steps for safeguarding your personal data, and there are many other resources available on the internet.

The following are a series of forms provided by the Office of the Inspector General that will be useful if, despite your efforts, you become a victim of identity theft:

- Chart your course of action.

- ID theft affidavit

- Fraudulent account statement

Section 5
Valuable Experience

Internships

Checklist for Searching for Internships

Community Service

Notes

Internships

The value of internships varies greatly depending on who you work for and the specific industry you have selected. If you deliver the coffee during a big meeting and glance up at the whiteboard before being shooed out of the room, did you really learn anything? Well, yes, if the words on the white board were "Secret Buyout by Google on Thursday". For the most part, though, interning in a college or a business can give you an understanding of what it is like to work in your chosen field.

There are however, some major benefits to interning. Certain majors require that you complete one or two internships prior to earning your graduate degree. Such was the case when I was studying for my graduate degree in counseling. Since my emphasis was College and Career Counseling, I was required to work as an intern in college counseling — that assignment was completed at the College of San Mateo. My second year was as an intern in career counseling at Stanford University.

Many other programs have similar requirements. Most of them are considered part of your education and usually do not provide financial compensation. Even though you work twelve to fourteen hours a week without a salary, some internships are very competitive. I was thrilled to be accepted at Stanford University because the learning opportunity was great, but it is also a plus to include that experience in my professional résumé. Does it make that much of a difference? You bet it does!

Remember:

*The best internships are the ones where you are
given real responsibility.*

Even if an internship is not a requirement for your major, it is still in your best interest to give serious consideration to completing one or two internships. If you can earn a small income while gaining valuable knowledge, it is so much the better.

I'm sure that you are aware of the very competitive job market that you will face once you have completed your education. It is essential to have some type of professional experience before you earn your degree. Internships are a wonderful vehicle to explore potential careers and an opportunity to gain very valuable experience working in a real-world professional environment.

Internships enhance your desirability as a candidate when job seeking in your chosen field. The experience prepares you to make more informed decisions and exposes you to professional contacts that will ultimately lead you to your dream career.

Note

*In some cases, your internship employer may offer you a permanent position if you
have shown that you are a
positive asset to their company or business.*

But for now know this; one of the more immediate benefits of doing an internship is increasing your potential for winning grants and scholarships. Anything that demonstrates your commitment to education makes you a more attractive candidate for winning financial awards. Companies and organizations want to help winners. Show by your actions and your grade point average (GPA) that you are the most promising applicant.

Checklist for Searching for Internships

☐ What is the organization looking for in a major or field of study?

☐ What are you looking for? Do you want something during the academic year or do you prefer a summer internship?

☐ What about location?

☐ How many hours a week can you dedicate without jeopardizing your grade point average?

☐ How long do you want to stay with one organization?

☐ Is there any compensation for your time? Any benefits?

☐ Do you want to work for a large or small firm?

☐ Do you need to be part of an academic program in order to qualify?

☐ What is the potential for permanent employment after graduation?

☐ Give the search a lot of thought and develop your own set of questions.

Community Service

Are you aware how important community service is? Well, let me tell you that it is big, really big. Not only is it important when applying for scholarships, but also four-year colleges are using it as admissions criterion. In addition, when you are ready to apply for your first job, your having participated in volunteer work will enhance your desirability as a candidate.

Of course, you need that little piece of paper to prove that you have obtained the educational background and are qualified for your dream career, but you need more than a college degree. Employers are looking for future leaders who have given their time to help those who are less fortunate.

The ideal type of community service relates in some way to your career, but finding the perfect volunteer work isn't always easy. At best, it will be more valuable to you if you participate in a service which is of interest to you. Do you prefer to work with children or seniors? Is there a cause that you are passionate about? There are many types of activities that qualify as community service and, I am sure, that you have participated in helping others without realizing it. In any event, you need to start documenting your service activities.

Many formal events such as AIDS marches, breast cancer awareness events, and fundraisers for the needy have publicity in local newspapers. Try to collect all of the data possible and, if you participated, request a letter as proof that you gave of your time.

One of the most wonderful forms of volunteerism is the Peace Corps. This program was initiated in the early sixties by President John F. Kennedy and continues to this day. I had the good fortune of being a part of this world-wide giving organization for five years. I didn't serve as a volunteer, but was the wife of an educational consultant in Liberia in West Africa and later the Peace Corps Director's wife in Ethiopia and Thailand.

The volunteers, who are college graduates, serve for a period of two years in developing countries. They are trained for about six weeks to become culturally acclimated to their foreign assignment and are taught the language of the host country.

The mission of the volunteers is to teach and work in remote villages and to act as personal ambassadors of good will. In the process each volunteer returns home with a better understanding of a different culture, but, more importantly, a better knowledge of him or herself. Although living conditions are basic in many instances, the experience is never forgotten and the Peace Corps Volunteers leave with more than they are given.

One of the beneficial results of joining the Peace Corps is that student loan repayment is put on hold until your two-year assignment is over. Another plus is the five or six thousand dollars that you are given to reenter the United States to reestablish yourself with a place to live and a job.

In short, being a volunteer is a good thing for those you serve and even a better thing for you. There is a glorious feeling that comes from knowing that you have made a positive difference in the world. We all need to have a purpose in life and giving to our fellow man is so rewarding.

By the way, if your circumstances do not permit you to travel abroad, there is a domestic version of Peace Corps known as AmeriCorps. Each year, AmeriCorps offers 75,000 opportunities for adults of all ages and background to serve as an AmeriCorps member. You can:

- tutor and mentor disadvantaged youth

- fight illiteracy

- improve health services

- build affordable housing

- teach computer skills

- clean parks and streams

- manage or operate after-school programs

- help communities respond to disasters

You might be interested in knowing that in 2009 the Senate passed the Serve America Act which was the work of Senator Edward Kennedy, who was President John F. Kennedy's youngest brother.

For your convenience, I have created a template for keeping track of your community service events. There is a sample at the end of this chapter, but you can actually download the template on www.findingmoneyforcollege.com which is my website. Once you are into the home page, just click downloads.

Overview:

You may meet people and participate in activities which you will never experience if you had not volunteered. In addition, it gives you a purpose in life.

Work and Life Experience:

Community Service is a great way to gain real world experience. It not only helps you to improve your skills in a field related to your future career goals, but it prepares you to communicate effectively and understand diverse philosophies of life.

Connections:

The contacts you make while volunteering can be a good source for letters of recommendation for college and scholarships. They can possibly help you in the future when you are looking for a paid position. Now is the time to start networking. Start by collecting and organizing business cards. It is a good idea to make notes on the back of the card about when, where and why you met the person. Who Knows? A volunteer contact could open the door to a wonderful career.

Community Volunteer Service Record

Event: _____

Location: _____ Date:_____

Number of Participants:_____ Hours Served: _____

What I Learned About Myself

_____

_____

_____

_____

_____

_____

_____

_____

_____

_____

_____

_____

_____

_____

_____

Community Service Scholarships

There are many scholarships available to students who want to make a difference in the world while enhancing their own credentials. There is nothing more rewarding than giving of your time to make the world a better place. Most people find that they receive more than they give.

At this stage in life, most of you are trying to reach your dream career goals. For many of you that means four to six years of formal education and staggering student loans. Those student loans will hamper your ability to buy a house or a car or provide for a family. College tuition and fees have grown way out of proportion making it nearly impossible to survive once you complete your studies.

The remedy is to learn how to submit winning scholarship applications and to win thousands of dollars in scholarship awards. The resources are out there. There are billions of dollars out there. The missing link is that there are many individuals who lack the interest and motivation to learn how to properly research and apply for scholarships.

Believe me — the money isn't just going to fall on your lap. You must work for it. It is much more than just filling out an application form and hastily writing a weak personal essay. Yes, there is money out there — lots of it, but the competition is also a challenge.

You have the opportunity to win scholarships for community service. In the process of giving of your heart and soul, you will gain self-confidence, meet amazing people in your community, discover motivating mentors, and you will be introduced to contacts that can open doors for you which lead to your future career.

The resources of scholarships are tremendous, but the following are specific for students who choose to volunteer. It is a small way that organizations can induce you to learn about yourself, serve others and to receive a scholarship of thanks. The benefits that you reap will go far beyond winning a scholarship. Remember that happiness cannot be bought, but it can be earned.

Community Service Scholarships

1. Alliant Energy Community Service Scholarship

Deadline: February 15th

Each year, Alliant Energy Foundation offers up to 25 Community Service Scholarships for $1,000 each to Midwest students who are enrolled full-time at an undergraduate institution within Iowa, Wisconsin, or Minnesota with a strong commitment for community leadership. Eligible candidates must be a current customer of one of Alliant Energy's utility subsidiaries, be 24 years of age or under, possess a cumulative GPA of 2.5 or higher, and submit a 250-word essay on recent volunteer activities.

Contact

Alliant Energy Community Service Scholarship
4902 North Biltmore Lane Suite 1000
Madison, WI 53718
(608) 458-0132
dlehtinen@scholarshipamerica.org

2. Angie Houtz Memorial Scholarship Fund

Deadline: April 30th

For students accepted to or currently enrolled in any two- or four-year public institution within Maryland, the Angie Houtz Memorial Scholarship Fund provides an annual scholarship for $3,000 to students with a strong community service background who have participated in at least two hundred hours of volunteer work in the last five years. Along with the application, candidates must include an official transcript, two-page typed essay on an indicated topic, three sealed letters of recommendation, and a comprehensive list of community service. (See: What Should be Included in a Letter of Recommendation on a College Scholarship Application?)

Contact

Angie Houtz Memorial Scholarship Fund

1450 Mercantile Lane Suite 207C

Largo, MD 20774

angiefund@yahoo.com

http://www.theangiefund.com/Scholarship.html

3. AXA Achievement Community Scholarship Program

Deadline: January 1st

With the mission of bringing access to higher education into every community nationwide, the AXA Foundation distributes up to twelve AXA Achievement Community Scholarships for $2,000 each to high school seniors who demonstrate strong ambition, determination, respect, academic achievement, and commitment to volunteer services. In addition, the program selects one outstanding student from each state, the District of Columbia, and Puerto Rico to receive a one-time community service scholarship for $10,000.

Contact

AXA Achievement Community Scholarship Program

1290 Avenue of the Americas

New York, NY 10104

(888) 292-4636

scholarship@axa.com

4. Bonner Scholars Program

Deadline: Varies

As a national philanthropic organization created by investor Bertram F. Bonner and his wife Corella in Princeton, New Jersey, the Bonner Scholars Program provides 4-year, $4,000 community service scholarships for up to 1,500 students enrolled at one of the 22 participating universities across the United States annually. In return for the financial support, recipients are required to commit at least 10 hours each week to volunteer work and participate in the foundation's summer community service internship experience.

Contact

Bonner Scholars Program
10 Mercer Street
Princeton, NJ 08540
(609) 924-6663
info@bonner.org

5. Comcast Foundation Leaders of Tomorrow Scholarship

Deadline: April 15th

In order to promote community service and build tomorrow's leaders, the Comcast Foundation Leaders of Tomorrow Scholarship program grants one-time awards for $1,000 to high school students who are nominated by their high school principals or guidance counselors in recognition of their community service, academic performance, and leadership potential. Eligible candidates must reside in a community served by Comcast, maintain a cumulative GPA of 2.8 or better, and be accepted to attend an accredited nonprofit U.S. institution.

Contact

Comcast Foundation Leaders of Tomorrow Scholarship
1701 JFK Blvd.
Philadelphia, PA 19103
(800) 934-6489
comcast@applyists.com

6. Disabled American Veterans Youth Volunteer Scholarships

Deadline: February 7th

Sponsored by the Department of Veterans Affairs, the Disabled American Veterans Youth Volunteer Scholarships program offers awards up to $20,000 to provide financial support for pursuing a higher education degree for young volunteers who are dedicated to serving disabled military veterans returning from service. Qualified applicants must have volunteered at least 100 hours at a VA medical center, be 21 years of age or under, and submit an essay on how volunteer work with veterans has impacted their academic/personal life.

Contact

Disabled American Veterans Youth Volunteer Scholarships
807 Maine Avenue SW
Washington, DC 20024
(202) 554-3501
VAVS@davmail.org

7. Disneyland Resort Celebrating Community Service Scholarship

Deadline: January 31st

The Disneyland Resort Celebrating Community Service Scholarship program awards 10 annual $7,500 scholarships to Orange County, California, high school seniors who demonstrate excellent leadership skills through the accumulation of 150 or more hours of volunteer work. Eligible applicants must be graduating high school seniors pursuing postsecondary education at a U.S. institution, have a minimum cumulative GPA of 3.0 or higher, and provide a letter of verification from the predominant, charitable, nonprofit organization with which they volunteered.

Contact

Disneyland Resort Celebrating Community Service Scholarship
P.O. Box 3232
Anaheim, CA 92803
(714) 781-0856
DLR.Community.Relations@Disney.com

8. Echoing Green Climate Change Fellowship Program

Deadline: February 1st

In partnership with the ZOOM Foundation, the Echoing Green Climate Change Fellowship Program provides an $80,000 stipend with health insurance to individuals who agree to participate in one year of professional development in community or humanitarian public service within the developing countries of the world. For consideration, qualified, next-generation, social entrepreneurs must demonstrate a commitment to working on innovations in mitigation and adaption to global climate change crisis.

Contact

Echoing Green Climate Change Fellowship Program
494 Eighth Avenue 2nd Floor
New York, NY 10001
(212) 689-1165
info@echoinggreen.org
http://www.echoinggreen.org/fellowship/climate-fellowship

9. Gloria Barron Scholarship for Young Heroes

Deadline: April 15th

In honor of an outstanding woman who devoted more than 20 years of her life to working at the Colorado School for the Blind, the Gloria Barron Scholarship for Young Heroes is granted to 25 inspiring, public-spirited, young leaders between the ages of 8 and 18 who have made a significant, positive difference to their communities and our environment. Winners of the $5,000 scholarship will receive a certificate of recognition, signed copy of "The Hero's Trail," and the opportunity to be paired with an adult mentor who is working in the winner's area of interest.

Contact

Gloria Barron Scholarship for Young Heroes
545 Pearl Street
Boulder, CO 80302
ba_richman@barronprize.org

10. Good Deeds Scholarship

Deadline: December 31st

Each year, the Good Deeds Scholarship awards $1,000 to students who submit the best winning, short 250-word essays discussing how their good deeds through volunteer work and community service have positively contributed to society to make a difference in the lives of others. At this time, the essay competition is only open to legal, English-speaking U.S. residents who are current high school students in their freshman, sophomore, junior, or senior year and are planning to enroll in an accredited postsecondary institution.

Contact

Good Deeds Scholarship
3020 Hartley Road Suite 220
Jacksonville, FL 32257
gooddeeds@scholarshipexperts.com

11. Heart of America Christopher Reeve Award

Deadline: November 7th

For those with the tendency to swoop in to help others like Superman, the Heart of America Christopher Reeve Award presents $1,000 annually to extraordinary middle or high school students who have demonstrated a tremendous amount of compassion and service to his or her local community. In order to be selected for the scholarship, eligible nominees must provide information about recent community service efforts with supporting documentation and professional reference letters.

Contact

Heart of America Christopher Reeve Award

1625 K Street NW Suite 400

Washington, DC 20006

(202) 347-6278

scholarships@heartofamerica.org

12. Kohl's Cares Scholarships

Deadline: March 14th

As one of the largest tuition assistance programs available for students who volunteer, the Kohl's Cares Scholarships program offers $1,000 to regional winners and $10,000 for national winners who are nominated based on the benefits and outcomes of their outstanding commitment to volunteer community service projects. Nominees must be between the ages of 6 and 18, have participated in volunteer efforts within the last year, submit a detailed list of community service efforts, and be nominated by an adult age 21 years or older.

Contact

Kohl's Cares Scholarships

17000 Ridgewood Drive

Menomonee Falls, WI 53051

(262) 703-7000

kohls@scholarshipamerica.org

13. Lowe's Charitable and Educational Foundation Scholarships

Deadline: December 15th

Annually, the Lowe's Charitable and Educational Foundation awards up to 140 scholarships for $2,500 each to high school seniors who are accepted for enrollment into an accredited U.S. undergraduate degree program full-time. Preference will be given to full- and part-time Lowe's employees with at least 90 days of service, their spouses/partners, and dependents.

Requiring a minimum cumulative GPA of 3.25 or higher, selection is based on academic performance, leadership potential, work experience, and community service involvement.

Contact

Lowe's Charitable and Educational Foundation Scholarships
1605 Curtis Bridge Road
P.O. Box 1111
Wilkesboro, NC 28697
(877) 665-6937
corpgc@lowes.com

14. Minnesota Historical Society Student Volunteer Services Scholarship

Deadline: February 14th

Administered by the Minnesota Historical Society (MNHS), the Office of Student Volunteer Services presents three scholarships for $1,000 each to high school seniors who are active members in good standing with the MNHS and have contributed at least 25 hours of volunteer work throughout the year. All eligible candidates must be between the ages of 15 and 18 years old, demonstrate financial need, and be committed to participating in the society's work.

Contact

Minnesota Historical Society Student Volunteer Services Scholarship
345 Kellogg Blvd. W
St. Paul, MN 55102
(651) 259-3188
volunteerservices@mnhs.org

15. National Caring Awards

Deadline: March 1st

Inspired by the example of Mother Theresa, the Caring Institute grants several National Caring Awards each year to individuals who are role models with an extraordinary dedication to community service and selfless concern for others. In order to receive the $2,000 award, young adults must be nominated before their graduation from high school or eighteenth birthday. All winners will be given an all-expenses paid trip to a special awards ceremony and VIP reception in recognition of entering the Caring Hall of Fame.

Contact

National Caring Awards
228 7th Street SE
Washington, DC 20003
(202) 547-4273
info@caring.org

16. Nestle Very Best in Youth Scholarship Competition

Deadline: July 1st

Created to spotlight the best in youth leadership and identify teens whose efforts are making a profound difference in our world, the Nestle Very Best in Youth Scholarship Competition is open to contestants between the ages of 14 and 18 years of age who demonstrate good citizenship, strong academic performance, and service to their school, church, or community. In order to be entered to win the $1,000 award, applicants must submit two letters of recommendation, a parent or legal guardian consent form, and an official transcript.

Contact

Nestle Very Best in Youth Scholarship Competition
800 North Brand Blvd.
Glendale, CA 91203
(818) 549-6677
NestleVeryBestInYouth@us.nestle.com

17. President's Volunteer Service Award

Deadline: Varies

Established in 2003 by the President's Council on Service and Civic Participation to recognize the significant contributions volunteers are making nationwide, the President's Volunteer

Service Award is one of the premier volunteer scholarships programs available to U.S. citizens. Open to kids ages 5 to 14, young adults ages 15 to 25, or adults over the age of 26, the award is offered at the bronze, silver, and gold level depending on the number of hours of volunteer service completed.

Contact

President's Volunteer Service Award
600 Means Street NW Suite 210
Atlanta, GA 30318
(866) 545-5307
inquiries@presidentialserviceawards.gov

18. Prudential Spirit of Community Awards

Deadline: November 5th

Sponsored by Prudential and the National Association of Secondary School Principals (NASSP), the Prudential Spirit of Community Awards are granted for $1,000 to $5,000 each to high school seniors accepted for enrollment in an undergraduate degree program who have continually engaged in community volunteer service. Eligible candidates are required to complete an application, write a personal statement on significant leadership contributions to community service, and submit a recommendation from the high school's principal.

Contact

Prudential Spirit of Community Awards
200 Crutchfield Avenue
Nashville, TN 37210
(615) 320-3149
spirit@prudential.com

19. Samuel Huntington Public Service Award

Deadline: January 18th

Established by the energy company National Grid, the Samuel Huntington Public Service Award is granted annually to graduating college seniors who wish to undertake one year of community service anywhere in the world before proceeding on to graduate school or a professional career. In order to qualify for the $15,000 stipend award, candidates graduating from a U.S. accredited institution must submit a one-page cover letter, service proposal, budget plan, official college transcript, resume, and three letters of recommendation.

Contact

Samuel Huntington Public Service Award
P.O. Box 11791
Newark, NJ 07101
(781) 296-8090
amy.stacy@nationalgrid.com

20. Sophia L. Gokey Scholarship Fund

Deadline: November 15th

In loving memory of American Idol alum Danny Gokey's wife, who devoted her short lifetime in touching the lives of children, the Sophia L. Gokey Scholarship Fund is designed to help youth achieve their higher education dreams despite significant roadblocks or setbacks from economic status. Eligible high school seniors for the $1,000 award must demonstrate accomplishments in community service and have a cumulative high school GPA of 2.7 or higher.

Contact

Sophia L. Gokey Scholarship Fund
2479 Murfreesboro Rd. Suite 515
Nashville, TN 37217
(800) 595-6269
http://www.sophiasheart.org/SophiaLGokeyScholarshipAward.php

21. Stephen J. Brady STOP Hunger Scholarships

Deadline: December 10th

Designed to recognize students who have made a significant impact on the national fight against hunger in America, the Stephen J. Brady STOP Hunger Scholarships are offered by the Sodexo Foundation to students between the ages of 5 and 25 who have demonstrated an ongoing commitment to their community by performing unpaid volunteer work eliminating hunger. Recipients will receive a $5,000 scholarship for their education and a matching grant in their name for the hunger-related charity of their choosing.

Contact

Stephen J. Brady STOP Hunger Scholarships
9801 Washingtonian Blvd.
Gaithersburg, MD 20878
(615) 320-3149
STOPHunger@sodexofoundation.org

22. Violet Richardson Award

Deadline: May 1st

Named after the president of the first Soroptimist club, the Violet Richardson Award is granted annually for $2,500 to honor young women who are making a difference in the world through participation in volunteer work, such as community service to end discrimination, fight poverty, assist women who are victims of domestic violence, or mentoring young girls. Eligible candidates for the award must be between the ages of 14 and 17 years old with a firm commitment to improving the lives of women and girls worldwide.

Contact

Violet Richardson Award
1709 Spruce Street
Philadelphia, PA 19103
(215) 893-9000
siahq@soroptimist.org

23. Washington Hospital Service League Volunteer Scholarships

Deadline: April 1st

Each year, the Washington Hospital Healthcare System presents the renewable Service League Volunteer Scholarships for $1,000 each to students in Fremont, Newark, Union City, and Hayward, California, who are pursuing an undergraduate degree in a health-related field. Qualified applicants must be U.S. citizens, be 22 years of age or younger, have been accepted to an accredited institution full-time, submit three letters of recommendation, and contribute to the community by accruing at least 100 hours of volunteer service annually.

Contact

Washington Hospital Service League Volunteer Scholarships
2000 Mowry Avenue
Fremont, CA 94538
(510) 797-1111
scholarships@whhs.com
http://www.whhs.com/community/scholarship-opportunities/

24. William R. Simms Award for Outstanding Youth in Philanthropy

Deadline: November 30th

In honor of one of the four founders of the Association of Fundraising Professionals (AFP), the William R. Simms Award for Outstanding Youth in Philanthropy is awarded to youth between the ages of 10 and 23 who demonstrate exemplary commitment to the community through direct financial support, volunteering, development of charitable programs, or leadership in philanthropy. Selection for the award is based on services conducted and long-term impact of the candidate's work on community members involved.

Contact

William R. Simms Award for Outstanding Youth in Philanthropy
4300 Wilson Blvd. Suite 300
Arlington, VA 22203

(703) 684-0410

kheyman@afpnet.org

25. Youth Service America Grants

Deadline: March 1st

Youth Service America (YSA) has established several grants ranging in value from $1,000 to $15,000 each in recognition of youth leaders between the ages of 5 and 25 who have voluntarily participated on projects that promote social change in their local or national communities. All recipients are expected to participate in the youth-led community service projects and celebration events on Global Youth Service Day and report on the impact of the activities.

Contact

Youth Service America Grants

1101 15th Street NW Suite 200

Washington, DC 20005

(202) 296-2992

info@YSA.org

Overall, participating in community service projects gives students the opportunity to form new personal connections, learn new practical skills, give back to communities in need, and possibly earn some extra scholarship funding for college. Whether you have started your own nonprofit organization fighting for a special cause or you only volunteer for a few hours each week, be sure to check out these 25 scholarships for community service and volunteerism to have some extra funding to afford the rising cost of achieving your higher education dreams.

Section 6
After You've Won

You're the Winner!! Now What?

Checklist/Dressing for Scholarship Acceptance

Go for More (Keep Applying)

Notes

You're a Winner!! Now What?

You filled out the application, submitted all of your documents before the deadline, you waited and waited for a response, and then the wonderful news that you were selected for a generous scholarship. Now you can relax. **NO WAY!!**

Before you do anything else, sit at the computer and write a thank you letter. It is not only the polite thing to do, but you might be eligible for another scholarship from the same organization at a later date. You must show your appreciation for being selected for financial assistance. The section on letters has a sample of a Thank You letter. Adapt it to fit your needs and mail it immediately.

Many of the college-based scholarships will require a thank you letter before they turn over your award check. That should tell you about the importance that is placed on acknowledging your appreciation. Everyone who has been involved in the process of assisting or writing on your behalf deserves a thank you.

Instructors and counselors will support you in any way that they can, but remember that at certain times of the year, faculty are inundated with requests for letters of recommendation. Sometimes this means a few extra hours a week from their already busy schedule. Please give thank you letters top priority — it spreads goodwill and makes you an attractive candidate for future scholarships.

Receiving a scholarship usually means that you will be invited to a luncheon or a dinner. The organization that is sponsoring you wants to show you off to the membership. You will be expected to say a few words, and you will be in the spotlight. Give careful consideration to your appearance. It is always safe to take a conservative approach and dress appropriately for the occasion.

Good grooming is a must! Dress as though you are going to a job interview. Take care not to use a fragrance that permeates the room, keep jewelry simple and be sure that your dress or suit is meticulously clean and pressed. Women should wear shoes that are appropriate for the dress — medium high heels in a conservative style. This is not the time for shoes that look like they belong in the bedroom or on the dance floor.

Men need to shave and have a hairstyle that is trim and freshly shampooed. Shoes need to be polished without worn down heels. Tattoos are best covered, and refrain from wearing jewelry other than a watch and perhaps one ring. Try not to call attention to any body piercing by eliminating earrings and other adornments. Although these are the fashion with younger people, it may not be favorably received by your scholarship sponsors. Try to be sensitive to the occasion and realize that many older individuals feel more comfortable with a conservative dress code. On a day-to-day basis, you can return to your individual manner of dress.

Checklist/Dressing for Scholarship Acceptance

WOMEN:

☐ Simple dress

   Avoid revealing necklines, tight, sexy styles, & short hemlines.

☐ Conservative shoes to coordinate with dress

☐ Meticulous grooming

   Clean, simple hairdo

   Makeup — simple (nothing theatrical)

   Clothes — clean and pressed

   Fragrance — subtle

   Shoes — polished without worn down heels

   Tattoos and/or body piercing — cover and minimize

   Fingernails — medium length with subtle polish

☐ Jewelry — keep to a minimum

☐ Accessories — coordinate with dress

☐ If you must wear a pantsuit, be sure that it is beautifully tailored.

MEN:

☐ Short sleeve shirt

☐ Slacks

   (If you live in the desert, a suit is not necessary.)

☐ Shoes — coordinate color with your slacks (socks should match your shoes)

☐ Belt — match your shoes

☐ Jewelry — limit to watch and one ring

☐ Fragrance — subtle

☐ Grooming

  Hair — recent haircut, freshly shampooed

  Beard — neatly trimmed

  Shower, shave, & deodorant

  Fingernails — cut and scrubbed

  Shoes — polished without worn down heels

☐ Tattoos and body piercing — covered and minimized

DO NOT WEAR SHORTS OR JEANS. IT IS BEST TO REFRAIN FROM UNUSUAL HAIR STYLES AND COLORS.

Go for More
(Keep Applying)

As long as you are in college, you need to keep researching and applying for scholarships, grants, and fellowships. The more scholarships you apply for, the better your chances will be for receiving a number of awards. In fact, receiving a scholarship will sometimes open the door for being selected for more financial assistance. Sponsors are interested in students who are deserving, and if another organization has found you worthy, it enhances your desirability.

I suggest that students start applying for scholarships when they are juniors in high school. Even if you decide to complete two years at a community college, you will have tuition fees and textbooks to purchase. Books have become so expensive that most of the time you will pay more for a text than you will for community college tuition.

Once you transfer to a four-year college, you will need greater financial resources. Tuition will be considerably higher even at a State University, and will increase dramatically if you attend a private college. For those students wanting to attend a private college, you will be faced with $40,000 to more than $100,000 for a four-year education. Scholarships are a vital part of paying for your education so it is important to learn the system of research and applying for awards.

By the time you complete your baccalaureate degree, you may owe money on student loans, and still face the need to enter graduate school. Are you beginning to get the picture about the need to continue to search for scholarships? Although an education is one of the best investments that you can make, it does make a considerable dent in your pocket.

Many students before you have been successful and there are many opportunities. Keep up your grade point average; stay committed to your educational goals; and continue your search for financial assistance. My very best wishes to you on your journey — I remain committed to help you in any way that I can.

Notes

Section 7
Money Management

Money
(Keeping What You Have)

Money Saved is Money Earned

Income and Expense Journal

My Monthly Budget

Money Saving Checklist

Notes

Money
(Keeping What You Have)

Winning scholarships is **great!** And by following **The Andrews System,** you will find money for college. The BIG question now is: "What are you doing about sheltering the money that you have?"

I have dedicated a number of pages further on in the book for managing your money, and I have even provided you with worksheets for setting up a budget — does the word budget make you want to run in the opposite direction?

Sorry, but I'm just trying to make the process easier for you. I think you will find them useful once you get used to the idea of analyzing your present system or lack thereof. I'm sure that you have heard of: "A penny saved…"

Yes, I know, you can't buy anything with a penny and a dollar doesn't buy much either. But, an accumulation of dollars starts to produce some buying power.

For now, I would like you to do some research on HOPE Scholarship and Lifelong Learning Credits. This could save you or your family up to $2,000 if you are eligible. It is definitely worth looking into when you file your taxes or discussing with your tax accountant.

Money Saved is Money Earned

On page 119, you were introduced to the HOPE Scholarship and the Lifetime Learning Credits. You also learned about using interest on student loans as a tax credit. Obviously, there are many ways to save money as well as scholarships to be earned.

For now, I would like to offer several suggestions for saving money. Start by visualizing yourself walking across that stage being handed your degree and realizing that you are very close to the career that you have been dreaming about. Every day hold that vision of yourself in a cap and gown receiving your degree. Exciting thought, isn't it?

That day will be here sooner than you realize and you can make it happen by winning scholarships and being frugal with your money. I know, I know, you're only young once and you have to have some fun. Yes, you do need to balance your hours of studying with some down time, but isn't it worth a few years of sensible spending?

You know, I have had many old (30 years old) students return to college after goofing off for a few years, and I have heard repeatedly, "I wish that someone had given me a kick in the pants." I suppose you have guessed by now that I am attempting to give YOU that kick in the pants. But, you will only get that message if you are ready to hear it.

Realistically though, for many students, earning $8.00 an hour takes priority over being a serious student. As a consequence, well-intended students start skipping class and not completing assignments because of demanding work schedules and busy social lives. Dropping out of classes and/or failing does not only spell disaster for your grade point average, but it means a loss of the tuition paid for your failed classes.

How about all of the money spent on junk food in the college cafeteria? I have seen students spend $10.00 a day on chips, French fries, Twinkies, and soft drinks. Do you realize that that adds up to $200 a month? Would you consider packing a lunch as a substitute? Not only would it save you money, but you would have a trimmer body.

Have you completed the FAFSA form? Do you qualify for the BOGW (Board of Governors Fee Waiver) that waives enrollment fees for qualified students?

Do you qualify for E.O.P.S. (Extended Opportunity Programs and Services) which is a state funded program that provides book vouchers, grants, support services and even laptop computers to high need, educationally disadvantaged students who are California residents?

Are you using a credit card indiscriminately and paying a high interest rate? If you must use a credit card, shop around for a lower interest rate. Many credit card companies are offering 0% interest for a limited time as an introduction. Be sure to charge only what you can pay in full the following month.

Are you buying things that you don't need? For necessary items are you doing comparative shopping at places like T.J. Maxx or Marshall's? Have you ever shopped at a Thrift store? I have found new or nearly new items for incredibly low prices. Several of my favorite pieces of clothing were purchased at Goodwill or Army Surplus stores.

Do you have any personal possessions that you no longer need that you can sell? Have you ever had a garage sale? Have you ever sold anything on e-Bay?

How about a special service that you can exchange for a product or service?

Is eating out too often diminishing your cash reserves?

Perhaps one of the biggest expenses that students incur is buying textbooks. I'm sure that you are aware that books are now costing more than tuition and paying $300 a semester for textbooks is not unusual. In the last year I have assisted students in buying books at a fraction of the retail price.

You need to have the ISBN number that is located on the back cover. Having the ISBN insures that you will have the right edition of the book. Professors are very specific about the publication date of the book.

Although there are numerous sources for buying and selling discounted college texts, there is a very recent one that is user friendly. On your computer, go to *www.schoolsoup.com*. Type in the ISBN number and the screen will display seven or eight sources of the book. Both new and used prices will be shown. If you click the vendor of the best price, you will see a description of the available books. I have personally purchased many used books from *www.bigwords.com* and have been very pleased. The wonderful thing is that my purchases have been like new.

I'm sure that you have some money saving tips. Give it some serious thought, and I'm positive that you will have some creative ideas of your own.

Income and Expense Journal

The first step toward "money smarts" for a college student is to set some financial goals. Although the main focus of this text is to find scholarships and grants to pay for tuition, textbooks, and other college related expenses, protecting the money that you presently have will allow you to be financially healthier when you complete your education.

For the next month keep a journal or log of all of your income and expenses. Keep track of every bag of chips, soda, French fries, parking fees, bridge tolls and charges on your credit card. In addition, keep a record of all long distance phone calls you make and how many minutes each call lasts.

After you record and analyze your spending habits, set up a realistic budget for yourself and stick to it. You will probably have some student loans when you receive your degree, but it is possible to control the amount of debt. Realize that once you have the career of your dreams, you can start earning and slowly purchase some of your wants.

Make four copies of the following expense log and record every penny spent. I know that it sounds like a bore, but the only way to know where your money is going is to keep track.

After a month, calculate the amount needed for a full semester.

My Monthly Budget

Education Expenses

Tuition and fees _____

Books and supplies _____

Health insurance _____

Housing

Room and board _____

Utilities (electric, gas, water) _____

Telephone _____

Cell phone _____

Food

COD cafeteria _____

Groceries _____

Restaurants _____

Beverages _____

Entertainment

Movies, plays, concerts _____

Cable TV _____

Sporting events _____

CDs _____

Recreation (equipment, fees) _____

Living Expenses

Clothing and shoes _____

Laundry/dry cleaning _____

Personal care (hair, toiletries) _____

Transportation Expenses

Car payment _____

Gas, oil and service _____

Auto insurance _____

Parking fees _____

Bus or taxi fare _____

Other Expenses

Computer/Internet access _____

Medical expenses _____

Loan payments _____

Subscriptions _____

Membership dues _____

Gifts _____

Total Monthly Expenses

_____

Money Saving Checklist

☐ HOPE Scholarship and Lifetime Learning Credits

☐ Attend classes and don't lose tuition fees

☐ Pack a lunch instead of buying junk food in the cafeteria

☐ Complete the FAFSA application

☐ Check with the E.O.P.S. office for eligibility

☐ Do you qualify for the BOGW?

☐ Shop around for a good interest rate on credit cards

☐ Buy only what you need

☐ Charge only what you can afford to pay in full the next month

☐ Do comparative shopping

☐ Have a garage sale

☐ Sell unnecessary items on e-Bay

☐ Exchange a skill or talent with other students

☐ Try not to eat out too often

☐ Check out the new user friendly website *www.schoolsoup.com*.

☐ Buy used textbooks through *www.bigwords.com* and *www.schoolsoup.com*

☐ Sell your books back when you finish your classes

Notes

Conclusion

Notes

The following tips summarize the message that has been presented in this book. I can't emphasize enough the importance of time management and organization. A system is necessary for being in control of all of the scholarships you will find and mailing (submitting) applications prior to the deadlines.

Wherever you live, I am just an e-mail away. Please feel free to contact me if you have any questions. You are my reason for developing this system and I remain dedicated to helping as many students as possible.

Good Luck in your search, Eve-Marie Andrews *www.eandrews@dc.rr.com.*

1. Complete the FAFSA form even if you don't think that you will qualify. Most scholarship applications require a copy of your SAR report.

2. If you can fit it into your schedule, take an Introduction to Scholarships class. You will learn a system that you can use through graduate school.

3. Write at least one PERSONAL STATEMENT. It should be reviewed several times. Have someone you trust read it. Ask your English teacher to read it. Be sure that it is free of typing and grammatical errors. Allow enough time.

4. Research scholarship books. Double check the scholarship on the Internet to be sure that it is current.

5. Research on the Internet. Many scholarship applications can be completed online.

6. Be mindful of deadlines. Don't miss out on money because of timing.

7. Follow directions exactly. Send only what is requested if specific documents are required.

8. You need at least three letters of recommendation. Ideally, your letters should be from counselors and instructors. Letters from family and friends are nice, BUT *not* for scholarship applications.

9. REMEMBER to *always* write a thank you for your letters of recommendation.

10. Set up a system for keeping track of your applications and deadlines.

11. The more scholarships you apply for, the more chances you have of winning. Don't limit yourself to your college scholarships.

12. Community service is a plus when applying for scholarships. Colleges are also favoring students who are involved in volunteer activities.

13. When writing your personal statement, try sticking to the point and give examples. Write the way you feel — show passion for your beliefs.

14. Send an application ONLY if you are eligible. You will be disqualified immediately if you don't meet basic requirements.

15. Try to understand the organization's goals for offering a scholarship. You will increase your chances of winning if you can direct your application to the sponsor's motivation.

16. Your application should be filled in completely. Make a note in the blank if the question does not relate to you — don't leave any blanks.

17. Neatness is very important. Ideally, your application will be typed. If that is not feasible, print carefully with a black pen.

18. Complete a scholarship résumé that lists your accomplishments.

19. Your name and the last four digits of you social security number should be on the upper right hand corner of every document.

20. If you need help, ask a professor or counselor to assist you in completing all documents.

21. Reflect pride in yourself by submitting a neat and well-organized application.

22. Start the application process a year before you enter the college of your choice.

23. If you find a wonderful scholarship, but have missed the deadline, file it in your portfolio for next year.

24. As a general rule, do not pay for a scholarship search — you can do more thorough research by taking a scholarship class.

25. If a fee is required to submit an application, pass it up unless it is a very attractive offer with a nominal fee. An exception might be the dues to join a professional organization in your field. If in doubt, check with your instructor or counselor.

26. **Keep searching all year long.** Encourage family and friends who are in high school to start searching in their **junior year.**

27. If applying for the Hispanic Scholarship Fund, have everything checked by your counselor before mailing. They are VERY particular about the materials submitted. Many qualified students have been rejected because they did not follow directions.

28. Keep your grade point average up — it does count for receiving scholarships.

29. You don't have to be poor to receive money for college. Many awards are based on merit.

30. There is a lot of scholarship money. If you are serious about your search, you WILL receive one or more scholarships.

31. Follow **The Andrews System** — you will get results.

Notes

Appendix

Application Status Sheet

Available Downloads

Personal Data Form

Scholarship Organizer for Portfolios

Worksheet for Scholarship Résumé

Notes

Application Status Sheet

Scholarship Information

• Scholarship Name	
• Contact Name	

• Award Amount		• Deadline	
• Address		• Phone	
		• Fax	
		• Email	
		• Website	

Application Information

• Date Submitted		• Submission Type	☐ Paper	☐ Electronic

• Documents Included	☐ Personal Statement ☐ Résumé ☐ Transcripts
	☐ Other

• Decision Date		• Renewable	☐ Yes	☐ No

References

• Reference Name	
	☐ Requested ☐ Received ☐ Thank You ☐ Mailed
• Reference Name	
	☐ Requested ☐ Received ☐ Thank You ☐ Mailed
• Reference Name	
	☐ Requested ☐ Received ☐ Thank You ☐ Mailed

Application Notes

Available Downloads

I created a number of forms for your convenience. If you go to my website *www.finding-moneyforcollege.com*, you can actually complete the information and then print a nice computer generated document. If you save the information, in a jiffy you can customize it for your next scholarship application. Neat and simple!!

Below is a description of the forms and how to use them:

◆ Scholarship Organizer

This sheet is vital for organizing all of your scholarships. You have an immediate view of all of the scholarships that fit your profile. Without an easy reference, it is difficult to keep up with all of your research.

◆ Application Status Sheet

This form is to be used as a cover sheet for a scholarship application that has been submitted. Before you mail or submit via e-mail, make a copy of all of the pages. Complete the Status Sheet and staple it to the top of your application copies. File in a separate binder for future reference and/or for follow up. If you reapply for that scholarship, most of your work is done.

◆ Personal Data Form

When requesting a Letter of Recommendation, submit a completed Personal Data Form; a copy of your transcripts; Guidelines for Writing a Letter; and scholarship requirements along with your request letter. This information will allow the recommender to write a credible letter on your behalf.

◆ Scholarship Résumé

Although scholarship applications don't usually require a Scholarship Résumé, you should have one in your portfolio to prevent a last minute scramble to produce one. This can also be used when requesting a Letter of Recommendation — it allows the writer to know you even better.

◆ Scholarship Résumé Sample

The Scholarship Résumé Sample is an example of what a scholarship résumé should look like.

◆ Guidelines for Letter of Recommendation

Include this sheet when requesting a Letter of Recommendation. It is important that any documents written on your behalf have a professional appearance. If the writer of the letter does not demonstrate credibility, your application could be rejected.

◆ My Monthly Budget

Some applications will request an accounting of your living expenses. This will provide that information in a professional-looking format.

◆ Labels for Your Portfolio

This is from the template for the insertable eight page dividers.

Personal Data Form

Personal/Scholarship Information			
• Name		• Date	
• Address		• Phone	
		• Student ID #	
• Email			
• Major and Career Goals			

Education/Interests/Travel			
• Plans for College, Trade School, or Special Training			
• Date of Graduation or Transfer		• GPA	
• Awards, Honors, Scholarships			
• Special Interests, Hobbies, Talents			
• Clubs and Organizations			
• Travel			

Financial Need			
• Financial Need			
• Who or What Inspired You to Pursue This Field			

Please return Letter of Recommendation by _____

Scholarship Organizer for Portfolio #1

Name of Scholarship	Source	Due	Sent	Notes
1.				
2.				
3.				
4.				
5.				
6.				
7.				
8.				
9.				
10.				

Scholarship Organizer for Portfolio #2

Name of Scholarship	Source	Due	Sent	Notes
11.				
12.				
13.				
14.				
15.				
16.				
17.				
18.				
19.				
20.				

Scholarship Organizer for Portfolio #3

Name of Scholarship	Source	Due	Sent	Notes
21.				
22.				
23.				
24.				
25.				
26.				
27.				
28.				
29.				
30.				

Scholarship Organizer for Portfolio #4

Name of Scholarship	Source	Due	Sent	Notes
31.				
32.				
33.				
34.				
35.				
36.				
37.				
38.				
39.				
40.				

Worksheet for Scholarship Résumé

Name
Street Address
City, State ZIP code
email address
phone number

Accomplishments	**Scholarships Won**
_____	_____
_____	_____
_____	_____
_____	**School/College Clubs**
_____	_____
Awards	_____
_____	_____
_____	_____
_____	**Talents**
_____	_____
Community Service	_____
_____	_____
_____	_____
_____	**Travel**
Honors	_____
_____	_____
_____	_____
_____	_____
Management Experience	**Work Experiences**
_____	_____
_____	_____
_____	_____
Off-Campus Organizations	_____
_____	_____
_____	_____
_____	_____
_____	_____

Index

146

9 780974 813349